General Editor:	David Jollands
Design Director:	Elwyn Blacker
Consultant Authors:	Paul Doherty
	Roy Edwards
	Alan Hibbert
	Jim Hudson
	John Little
	John Mason
	Cleland McVeigh
	Peter Metcalfe
	Beverley Moody
	Patrick Moore
	Michael Pollard
	Keith Porter
	Tim Pridgeon
	Derek Slack
	Ian Soden
	Tony Soper
	Alan Thomas
Research Editor:	Simon Jollands
Design and Production:	BLA Publishing Limited
	Michael Blacker
	Simon Blacker
	Margaret Hickey
	Alison Lawrenson
	Graeme Little
	David Oakley
	Lorrie Spooner
Artists:	Paul Doherty
	John Flynn/Linden Artists
	Hayward & Martin
	Richard Lewis
	Steve Lings/Linden Artists
	Jane Pickering/Linden Artists
	Chris Rotheroe/Linden Artists
	Eric Thomas
	Brian Watson/Linden Artists
	Phil Weare/Linden Artists
	Rosie Vane-Wright

CAMBRIDGE SCIENCE UNIVERSE

PATTERNS OF LIFE ON EARTH

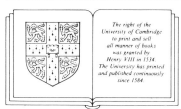

The right of the
University of Cambridge
to print and sell
all manner of books
was granted by
Henry VIII in 1534.
The University has printed
and published continuously
since 1584.

CAMBRIDGE UNIVERSITY PRESS

Cambridge · London · New York · New Rochelle · Melbourne · Sydney

Acknowledgements

The publishers wish to thank the following organizations for their invaluable assistance in the preparation of this book.

Airships Industries (UK) Ltd
Austin Rover Group Ltd
British Caledonian
British Hovercraft Corporation Ltd
British Petroleum
British Robot Association
British Telecom
Canon (UK)
Central Electricity Generating Board
Cincinnati Milacron Ltd
Commodore (UK) Ltd
Disabled Living Foundation
Dundee University
Eaton (UK) Ltd
Ferranti plc
Ford Motor Company
Furuno Ltd
General Electrical Company plc

Japan Ship Centre
Kodak Museum
Longines
NASA
National Film Board of Canada
Omega Electronic
Philips International bv
The Plessey Company plc
Rediffusion Simulation Ltd
Rolls-Royce Ltd
Royal Greenwich Observatory
Royal Smeets Offset
Shell
Sony (UK)
Southern Positives and Negatives (SPAN)
Standard Telephones and Cables
United Nations Organization
US Information Service

Published by the Press Syndicate of
the University of Cambridge,
The Pitt Building, Trumpington Street,
Cambridge CB2 1RP
32 East 57th Street, New York, NY 10022, USA
296 Beaconsfield Parade, Middle Park,
Melbourne 3206, Australia

© BLA Publishing Limited 1984

First published 1984

Library of Congress Catalog Card Number: 83-25253

British Library Cataloguing in Publication Data

Cambridge science universe.
Vol. 8: Patterns of life on Earth
1. Science — Juvenile Literature
I. Jollands, David
500   Q163

ISBN 0-521-26004-3

This book was designed and produced by
BLA Publishing Limited, Swan Court,
East Grinstead, Sussex, England.

Also in LONDON · HONG KONG · TAIPEI · NEW YORK · SINGAPORE

A Ling Kee Company

Phototypeset in Great Britain by
Southern Positives and Negatives (SPAN).
Colour origination by Chris Willcock Reproductions,
Premier Graphics and Planway Ltd.
Printed and bound in The Netherlands by
Royal Smeets Offset BV, Weert.

Photographic credits

t = top   b = bottom   l = left   r = right   c = centre

Cover photographs: *tl, tc, tr, bl* ZEFA; *br* Stephen Dalton/NHPA

Title page: ZEFA

4*c* Jany Sauvanet/NHPA; 4*b* Biofoto Associates/NHPA; 5 ZEFA; 6 Institute of Geological Sciences; 7 M. Walker/NHPA; 8*t*, 8*b* Institute of Geological Sciences; 9, 10*t*, 10*cb* ZEFA; 11 Michael Holford; 12 ZEFA; 13*tl*, 13*tr*, 13*cl* Biofoto Associates/NHPA; 14 M. Walker/NHPA; 15 Stephen Dalton/NHPA; 16, 17*tl* ZEFA; 17*tr*, 17*bl*, 18*bl* Keith Porter; 18*t*, 18*br* ZEFA; 19*cr* Brian Hawkes/NHPA; 20 ZEFA; 21 Stephen Dalton/NHPA; 22*t*, 22*b*, 23*t*, 23*cl*, 23*br* ZEFA; 23*cr* Keith Porter; 24*b*, 25*t* ZEFA; 25*r* Ivan Polunin/NHPA; 26, 27*tl* ZEFA; 27*r* James Tallon/NHPA; 28*t* Keith Porter; 28*c* G. J. Cambridge/NHPA; 29*l* E. Hanumantha Rao/NHPA; 29*br* ZEFA; 30*bl* L. Campbell/NHPA; 30*br* Stephen Dalton/NHPA; 30*cr* Keith Porter; 31*tr*, 31*cl* Anthony Bannister/NHPA; 31*b* R. J. Erwin/NHPA; 32*l* ZEFA; 32*r* Keith Porter; 33*bl* Bill Wood/NHPA; 33*br* ZEFA; 34*t* Keith Porter; 34*bl* A. Barnes/NHPA; 34*r* ZEFA; 35*t* Stephen Dalton/NHPA; 35*r* G. J. Cambridge/NHPA; 36*cl* J. & A. Sauvanet/NHPA; 36*tr* Peter Johnson/NHPA; 36*br* Don Pavey; 37 James Carmichael/NHPA; 38*bl* Stephen Dalton/NHPA; 38*t* S. Krasemann/NHPA; 39*t* ZEFA; 39*b* Peter Johnson/NHPA; 40*l* ZEFA; 40*r* Anthony Bannister/NHPA; 41*tl* Stephen Dalton/NHPA; 41*bl* Aquila Photographics; 41*br* George Bernard/NHPA; 42*bl* ZEFA; 42*br* Stephen Krasemann/NHPA; 43*tl*, 43*br* ZEFA; 43*tc* Anthony Bannister/NHPA; 44*l*, 44*r*, 44/45, 45*cr* ZEFA; 45*tr* Stephen Krasemann/NHPA; 46, 47*cl* ZEFA; 47*b* Mansell Collection; 50, 54, 55*t*, 55*b* ZEFA; 56*t* Y. J. Rey-Millet/World Wildlife Fund; 56*bl*, 57*bl*, 57*br* ZEFA; 57*tr* E. A. Janes/NHPA; 58*l* Mansell Collection; 58*t* K. Ghani/NHPA; 59*tl* E. Hanumantha Rao/NHPA; 59*tr* Lacz Lemoine/NHPA; 59*cr* Peter Johnson/NHPA; 59*bl* David Manners/NHPA; 60 ZEFA; 61 Stephen Dalton/NHPA.

Contents

NOTE TO THE READER: while you are reading this book you will notice that certain words appear in **bold type**. This is to indicate a word listed in the Glossary on page 62. This glossary gives brief explanations of words which may be new to you.

Introduction

THE VARIETY OF LIFE on our planet is immense, ranging in size from microscopic particles called **viruses** to the giant Californian redwood trees, which can grow to a height of 90 m. In between these extremes are found a great range of different plants and animals. All of these provide interest and mystery in the world around us. Despite the variety, all forms of life are made up from the same basic chemicals, and they all depend upon water and oxygen for their continued survival.

This variety of life would be impossible to understand without some kind of order, or **classification**. From the earliest times, humans have tried to classify life in the surrounding **environment**. Stone Age man, for example, would

probably have divided living organisms into those which could be eaten and those which should be avoided. We know that the early Greeks recognized broad groups of the larger animals but placed all snails, insects and other small life forms into a group they called 'worms'. Today we split all living organisms into two main groups, or **kingdoms**, which we call plants and animals. This division is a very important one and is based upon the way organisms obtain their food. Most plants contain coloured chemicals which are able to trap the energy of sunlight, and they use this to make sugars. Animals are not able to feed in this way, but instead they need to feed on plants, or other animals.

An important classification term is the **species**. This is the name given to groups, or

The three-toed sloth is a very strange animal. It feeds on leaves, hanging upside down from branches. The sloth travels slowly along the branches, moving one foot at a time. Its claws have become hooks, and its hair grows in the opposite direction to that of other animals. This lets the rain drain away when it is upside down.

Viruses are so small that they can only be seen through a very powerful microscope. They are the smallest living organisms of all, and cause many diseases, including the common cold.

populations, of organisms which look very similar. They are able to breed with one another, and so **reproduce**, or continue their species. The idea of a species is not new to any of us. From the early days of childhood we learn the difference between a lion and a tiger, or a dog and a cat. We know from the evidence of animal and plant remains, or **fossils**, that species change with time. Some species are not able to change or **adapt** to new environments and may die out and become **extinct**. The sabre-toothed tiger, for example, which chased our ancestors who lived in caves, does not exist today. It became extinct as the modern tiger, puma and other large cats developed.

When a species does adapt, the process of change is called **evolution**. Animals and plants may gradually change their habits, shapes and even colour to compete with a changing world. The locality in which a plant or animal lives is called a **habitat**. Each species learns to use its particular habitat to the fullest. To do this, species have to avoid animals which prey on them, and they have to fight against, or compete with, species similar to themselves. This continual fight for survival has been going on since life first evolved and still takes place today.

To avoid excessive competition, each individual species of animal and plant occupies its own **niche** within the environment. For example, two species of flamingo live on the shores of Lake Nakuru in Kenya. The two populations intermingle and compete for living space. However, they do not compete for food, each species feeding on different things in the same environment. Each species exploits a particular niche. In this way, the habitat is used to the fullest.

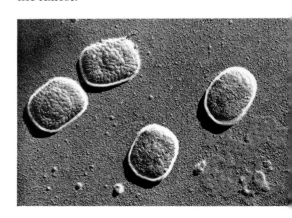

The beginning of life on earth

Diatoms, a kind of algae, are microscopic plants, found near the surface in lakes and seas. They reproduce by dividing into two parts. Diatoms are very important as the basis of food on which fish depend *(right)*.

WHAT DO WE MEAN by life? Looking around the world we see a large variety of living **organisms**. All these organisms have one thing in common – they are all built from units called **cells**. Each cell is much like any other, and contains the same basic structures and chemical **molecules**. We think that the first life form on Earth was a very simple sort of cell. This cell would have needed a cell wall, or **membrane**, to contain and protect all the complicated molecules needed for life.

These molecules all contain the element carbon, and they are called **organic** compounds. Sugars, fats and **proteins** are all examples of organic compounds. Such materials do not exist in the rocks, soil or air of Earth. Some of the organic compounds that make up cells are themselves made from simple building blocks called **amino acids**. These compounds are called proteins. Before the first simple cell could have existed, these basic units would have needed to be present on Earth. The key to understanding the beginnings of life on Earth lies in finding how these amino acids were first formed.

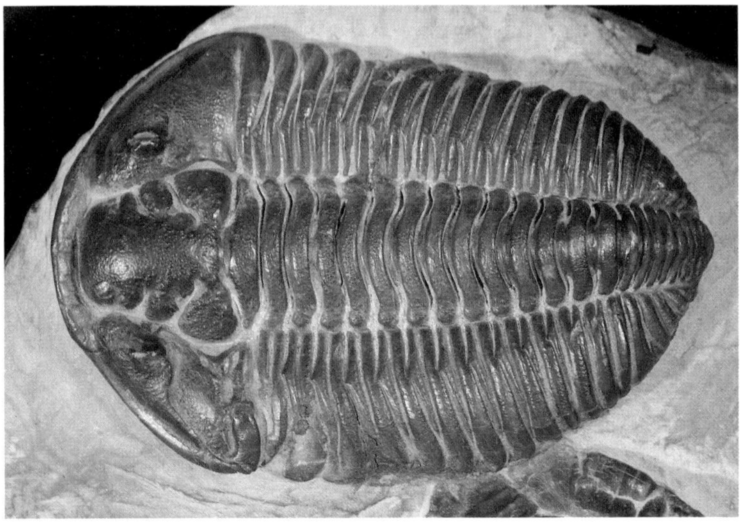

Fossils of trilobites, like this one *(above)*, are found in rocks 500 million years old. The trilobite was a marine animal similar to a woodlouse.

The Earth on which life began was a very different place from the one we know today. The air, or **atmosphere**, is thought to have been composed of a mixture of gases called **methane, ammonia** and water vapour. An atmosphere of this type exists on the planet Jupiter today. This atmosphere was slowly changed to one made from **carbon dioxide, nitrogen** and water vapour. Neither kind of atmosphere is able to

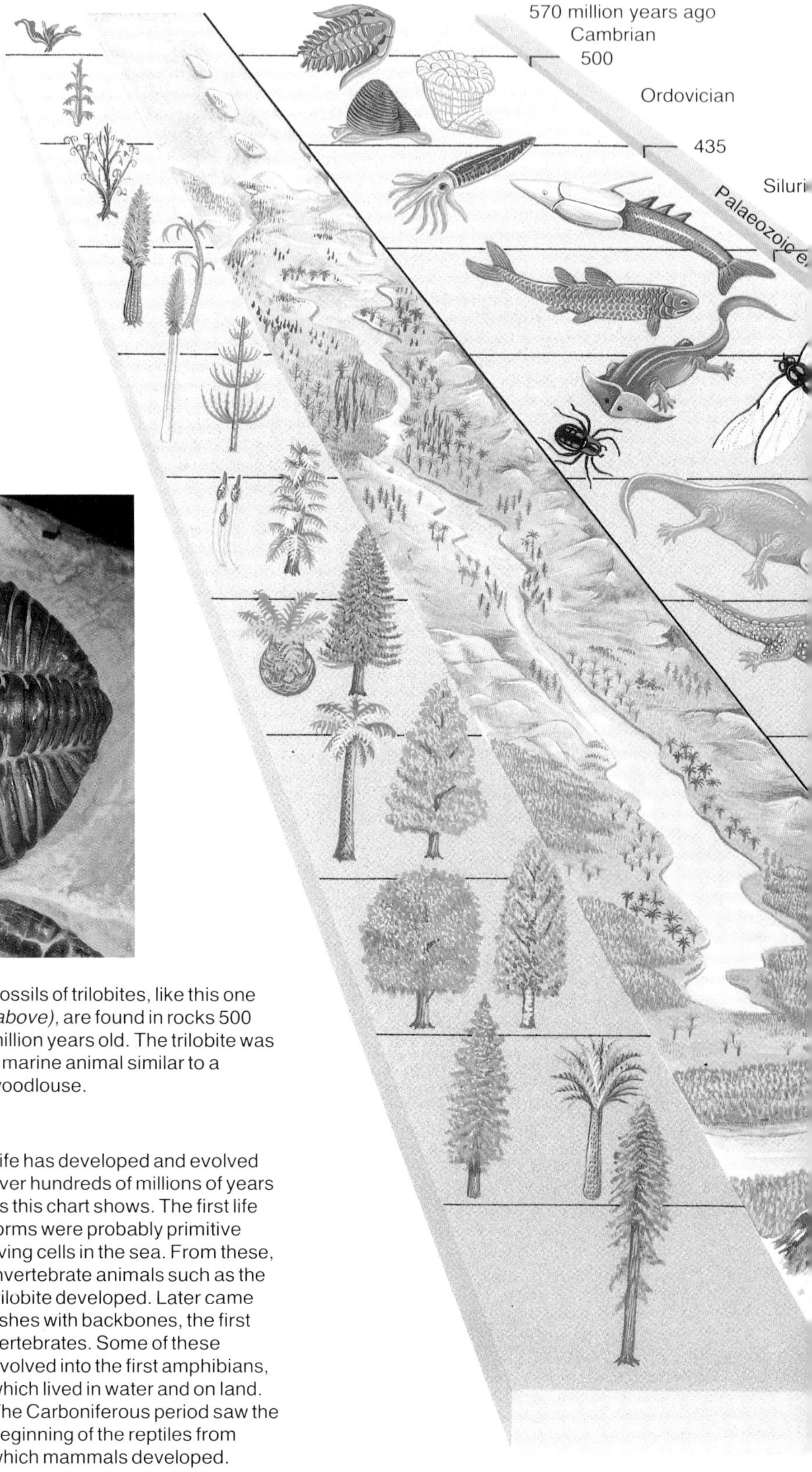

570 million years ago
Cambrian
500
Ordovician
435
Siluri
Palaeozoic e

Life has developed and evolved over hundreds of millions of years as this chart shows. The first life forms were probably primitive living cells in the sea. From these, invertebrate animals such as the trilobite developed. Later came fishes with backbones, the first vertebrates. Some of these evolved into the first amphibians, which lived in water and on land. The Carboniferous period saw the beginning of the reptiles from which mammals developed.

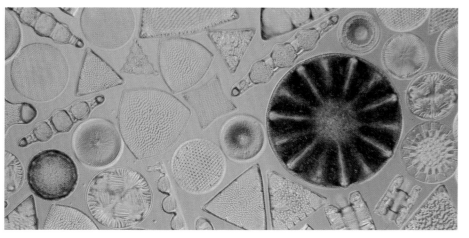

Sun by water, the first simple cells would have developed in the lakes or seas of the young Earth. These first cells were far too small and soft to be preserved as **fossils**, but the organic compounds they were made of still remain. These are called **chemofossils** and have been found in rocks 4000 million years old. We think the first cells preserved as fossils are in a rock called **fig tree chert** found in Swaziland in southern Africa. These rocks contain microscopic cells very like modern **bacteria**. These early forms of life used sunlight to help them make food. The process they used was probably similar to that carried out by green plants today. We call this process **photosynthesis**. A byproduct of photosynthesis is the gas oxygen. Once this began to build up in the atmosphere, a special type of oxygen called **ozone** began to block out all the harmful radiation from the Sun. Only the gentle sunlight as we know it today managed to filter through. Then life could move up to the surface of water and eventually on to land.

prevent harmful radiation from the Sun from reaching the Earth's surface. Even so, scientists think that these high-energy rays helped to create the first amino acids and thus the simple organic molecules needed for life. This has been shown in the laboratory by passing electric currents and radiation into mixtures of the gases named above. Since the first experiments in 1950, scientists have managed to produce a number of the simple organic molecules needed to build the first cells.

Protected from the harmful radiation of the

As cells became more complicated and their variety increased, the first **multicellular** organisms began to appear. Eventually, over long periods of time, new types of plants and animals evolved. Animal types developed new methods of feeding which made them dependent on plants. Later some animals began to feed on other animals and so, gradually, different **food chains** began to develop.

This is how we think life began. Parts of the story may be wrong, but the overall idea is probably accurate. Perhaps we may never know the whole truth. Despite the mystery of how life began, we can follow the development of the variety of life forms around us today by studying fossils of previous types. The simple forms of life of millions of years ago have given rise to the endless variety of life on Earth today.

ian

345

Carboniferous

280

Permian

230

Triassic

195

Mesozoic era

Jurassic

140

Cretaceous

65

Tertiary   Palaeogene

Neogene

Cenozoic era   1.8 million years ago

Quaternary

How life developed

THE WORLD HAS NOT always been as we know it today. Continents have moved, ice-ages have come and gone, and mountains have been raised up and worn away. During all these changes, living organisms have had to **adapt** to their changing environment. They have done this by altering their shape, size or way of life to suit the changing conditions. This process of adaptation takes place very slowly. Thousands of years have been needed for even a small part of an animal or plant to change. This process is called **evolution** and it is still taking place in the world today.

Many of the ancient species of plants and animals were not able to adapt to changes in their environment and they died out, or became **extinct**. The dinosaurs are an example of this. We learn about these early plants and animals from their fossil remains, left in rock. The hard bones and teeth of many animals were strong enough to avoid being crushed to powder when the ancient mud containing them gradually changed into rock. Plant fossils are much rarer, because they lacked hard tissue. Instead, we find copies, or **impressions**, of plants left in fine-grained rock and coal deposits.

From such evidence, scientists know that the very first life forms were simple plants, similar in some ways to the blue-green **algae** and **bacteria** of today. The first living cells appeared in the

Ammonite fossils are found in rocks all over the world. They vary in size from that of a small pea to that of a bicycle wheel. Ammonites became extinct at the end of the Cretaceous period.

During the Carboniferous period much of the earth was covered by warm, swampy forests. Giant ferns, growing to a height of 25 m, horsetails, and the first cone-bearing trees were typical of this period. .

seas and waters of the world. It was not until 395 million years ago that the first plants grew on land. To do this, they needed to develop, or evolve, roots and stems to support their sun-seeking leaves. These early land plants included huge ferns, some growing to a height of 25 m. They reproduced by forming **spores**, as do the ferns of today. Forests of huge ferns, horsetails and the first **conifers**, or pine trees, thrived some 340 million years ago in the hot swamps of the world. The remains of these plants gradually sank beneath the mud and **fossilized**, to form deposits of coal, which we use today as fuel.

An important change in plant evolution came about 100 million years ago when flowering plants began to appear. These seed producing plants adapted more easily to changing conditions than did other groups of plants. As a result, flowering plants became the dominant group 65 million years ago, and have remained so to the present day.

600 million years ago   500

Footprint of a dinosaur in sandstone–Connecticut State Park, USA.

The development of life on Earth spans hundreds of millions of years. We are vertebrates, that is to say we have backbones. The first vertebrates were fish. Some early species of fish became amphibians and were able to live on land and water. Reptiles developed from these amphibians, but only the smaller species survived. Some of these evolved as mammals, others as birds.

In the early seas, tiny, single-celled animals fed on plants and evolved in a variety of different ways. Some, like the first sponges, fed by **sieving**, or straining, tiny plants from the seawater. Others, such as the **trilobites**, organisms similar to woodlice, lived on the seabed. They probably fed on the rotting remains of animals and plants.

These first animals were all **invertebrates**, meaning that they lacked a stiff backbone. These organisms gave rise to a variety of crabs, corals, snails, worms and other groups. One of the most important stages in the evolution of invertebrates was the move on to land from the seas. This led to the evolution, 380 million years ago, of a very successful group, the insects. They followed plants on to the land, developing a tough, waterproof outer skeleton, or **cuticle**. This adaptation has resulted in the insects becoming one of the most successful group of land animals.

Animals with backbones, the **vertebrates**, form the other main division of the animal kingdom. They began as fish-like organisms in the oceans, 465 million years ago. By 345 million years ago they had evolved as true fish with jaws. This adaptation allowed this new group to feed on other animals. As these early fish increased in size, some of them developed lungs for breathing air. Lungs allowed them to move on to land. Some of these air breathers became better adapted to life on land, and gradually gave rise to **amphibians**. These animals had soft bodies and webbed skins. Although they could breathe air, they had to return to water to breed. From these soft-skinned amphibians, the first **reptiles** developed.

Reptiles had a hard body-covering of bony plates for protection, and the eggs they laid had a covering of shell. These adaptations made it possible for the reptiles to move away from the water and occupy the land. By 270 million years ago the reptiles had greatly increased in size and were thriving. The dinosaurs became the dominant group. This lasted until 65 million years ago when the dinosaurs became extinct. Scientists do not know why this happened, but it is thought that a very cold period in the history of the Earth may have been responsible.

At the same time as the reptiles were developing, another group of animals was beginning to evolve. This was the birds, and their earliest fossil remains are found in rocks about 150 million years old.

The first **mammals**, resembling tiny, shrew-like animals, survived this disaster period. Mammals have survived successfully because they are warm-blooded, and continue to protect their young until old enough to survive in the world. The first mammals gave rise to the variety of large animals which dominate Earth today.

400	300	200	100	60

Human beginnings

ALL THAT IS KNOWN about the origin of mankind has been learned by studying pieces of bone preserved as fossils in rocks. Our ancestors were not as numerous or widespread as people are today. As a result of this, their fossils are very rare. As our early ancestors developed, they began to use tools, some of which have been found. We see these tools as evidence of their presence. These tools and the remains of meals, such as animal bones or seeds, tell us much about the way in which our ancestors lived.

Humans belong to an animal group known as the **primates**. This group includes monkeys, apes, and two small groups of monkey-like animals called **lemurs** and **tarsiers**. All primates have long arms and legs, which help them to move through trees. Their hands and feet each have four fingers or toes, and a larger thumb or big toe, all known as **digits**. They are perfectly adapted for clinging on to and gripping branches or holding food. Good eyesight is very important to tree-dwellers, and most primates have forward-facing eyes. These help them to judge distances before leaping from branch to branch. The primates also have large brains, and this is a key to the success of our own evolution.

The oldest known fossils of primates have been found in rocks almost 70 million years old. These fossils suggest that the animals themselves looked more like shrews than monkeys. However, by 55 million years ago, a whole range of new primates had developed from them. Among this group were the first apes, the fossils of which have been found in Africa. They are thought to have been tree-dwellers and to have fed on soft fruits and leaves. This has been suggested because their fossilized teeth and skeletons look like those of the fruit-eating monkeys of today.

About 15 million years ago, the climate changed. This, in turn, affected the landscape of Africa. The forests, where the first apes lived, began to disappear and the country became drier and more open. This forced the apes to become ground-dwellers and to eat roots and tough seeds. This change in diet is shown in fossils by the development of large **molar** teeth, used for grinding. Also, some of the more advanced apes began to walk upright on their hind legs.

Our first semi-upright fossil ancestor has been discovered in rocks about 5 or 6 million years old. The name given to this fossil is *Australopithecus*. This means 'southern ape' because the first fossils were found in southern Africa. *Australopithecus* was about 1.6 m tall and had a small brain. Its tooth pattern suggests that it may have been a meat eater, but scientists are not certain about this.

Much of the information about our early ancestors comes from the tools and refuse they left behind them. This fossilized bone *(above)* shows the marks of a Stone Age cutting tool.

The people of the new Stone Age in northern Europe buried their dead in tombs and huge burial mounds *(right)*. At about the same time, the Egyptians were burying their dead in pyramids of stone.

Some scientists think that our next direct ancestor developed from *Australopithecus*. This more recent ancestor, named *Homo habilis*, used tools of stone or bone to kill and cut up animals for food. This ancestor is considered to be the first hunter. Remains have been found in rocks which are 2 million years old, revealing a larger brain than that of *Australopithecus*, and a tooth pattern similar to that of modern humans.

About 1.5 million years ago, another type of

Scientists still do not know for certain how the modern human *Homo sapiens* evolved. Some believe that we are more directly descended from *Homo erectus*, and that Neanderthal man is of lesser importance in the line of ancestors.

ancestor appears in the fossil records. This fossil has been given the name *Homo erectus* because its fossil skeleton shows that it walked upright. Its brain was smaller than ours, and its skull was quite a different shape. Fossils of *Homo erectus* have been found as far apart as Africa,

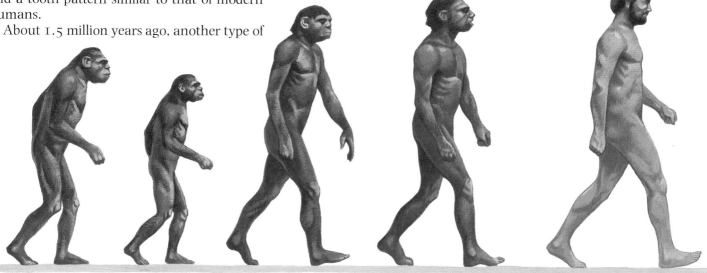

| Australopithecus | Homo habilis | Homo erectus | Neanderthal man | Homo sapiens |

China and southern Europe. It was a skilful hunter, able to kill large animals with spears and stones.

In Europe and the Middle East, some 70 000 years ago, another type of ancestor began to appear. Scientists have named the fossil remains Neanderthal man. This had a larger brain than previous forms, and was short and stocky in shape. We know much about the group represented by Neanderthal man because some made greater use of tools and buried their dead.

Alongside remains of Neanderthal man, the first signs of modern human beings appeared, some 60 000 years ago. The name that we have given to ourselves is *Homo sapiens*, meaning wise man, because of our large brains and our intelligence. The first modern humans had rounded skulls, with high foreheads, and small chins, and would have looked much like present-day humans.

The rest of human development is a matter for history. We have developed because of our superior brains. These have allowed us to gain partial control of our own environment, so separating us from the rest of the living world. This degree of independence from the rest of life is one reason why humans are different from other animals. Human beings are able to **reason**, or think, and this has made us the most adaptable, intelligent, and deadly of animals.

Life on the microscale

WE LIVE IN A WORLD which contains a wide variety of animals and plants. These in turn show a great range in size. Many organisms are microscopic and some of these consist of only one cell. Other microscopic organisms are made of a number of cells. Even the smallest insect, a mere millimetre or so long, is made of thousands of cells.

The cell is the basic building unit of all life forms. Cells vary in size. Some cells are so small that several thousand are needed to cover an area the size of a pinhead. Other cells are big enough to be just visible with the naked eye. Until the **microscope** was invented, we knew nothing about cell structure. The first people to look down microscopes were amazed to see huge numbers of tiny organisms in drops of pond water.

When we first see single-celled organisms it is often difficult to decide whether they are plants or animals. One way of deciding is to look at their colour. Single-celled plants, such as algae, are usually green or brown in colour. This is due to the pigment called **chlorophyll**, used by all plants to trap the energy of sunlight.

One of the first simple pond animals to be seen by early investigators was the single-celled **amoeba**. Biologists have decided that the amoeba is an animal and they classify it in the group called **protozoa**. We group the amoeba as an animal rather than a plant because it catches other single-celled animals and plants for food.

All single-celled organisms, whether they are plants or animals, are found only in water or moist places. They would quickly dry out and shrivel up if removed from water. Some move using tiny hairs called **cilia**, which beat together to 'paddle' the tiny organism through the water. Others have long microscopic whips, or **flagellae**, which work like a propeller to push the plant or animal cell through the water. The simple amoebae have an unusual way of moving. They seem to flow over the surface rather like raindrops running down a window-pane.

Small though they are, the single-celled plants and animals are large in comparison with some other types of organisms. These are the bacteria and viruses. Bacteria have thick, tough, outer walls and a regular shape. They can be shaped like tiny balls, rods or even spirals. They are present in soil, water and in the air we breathe. Many diseases in animals are caused by bacteria. These include typhoid, pneumonia and tonsillitis. Such diseases are caused not by the bacteria as such, but by their waste products, which are poisonous to animal cells.

Not all bacteria are harmful to humans.

If you were to examine a drop of ocean water under a powerful microscope, you would see a variety of beautifully-shaped organisms. These are the protozoa which make up plankton, on which other species feed. Those in the photograph below are called foraminifera. They have shells made of glass-like material, and are so tiny that twenty or more could fit on a pinhead.

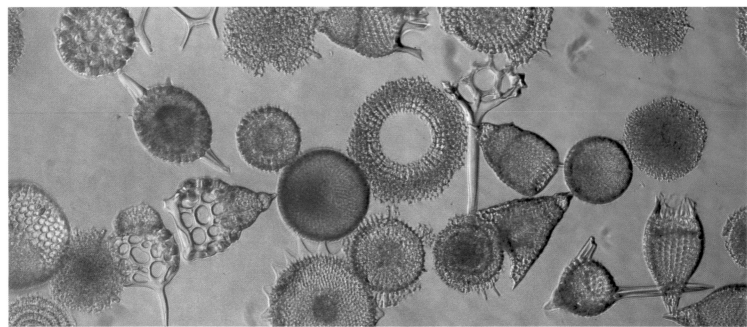

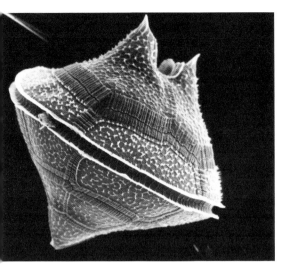

Viruses are so small that we need an electron microscope to see them. They are much smaller than bacteria, and can only grow inside living cells. Viruses attack animals and plants, and even bacteria.

They vary considerably in size. The larger they are (as seen left), the more complicated is their structure. On the right is a group of viruses *(adenovirus)* magnified 100 000 times. These appear as symmetrical polygons, as do many of the smallest life forms.

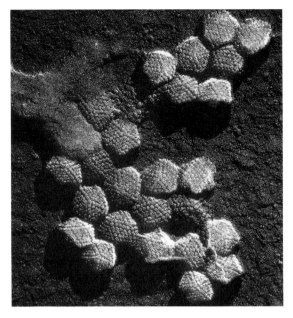

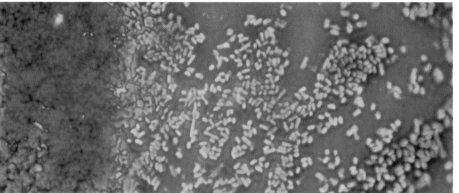

Cholera is a dangerous disease caused by drinking polluted water. The cholera bacteria is seen above.

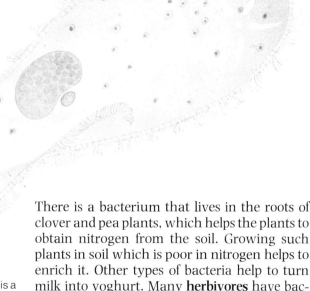

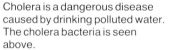

Paramecium, magnified x700, is a single-celled organism. It moves through water by waving hairs, called cilia, to and fro. Cilia are also used to sweep food particles in through a food gullet.

There is a bacterium that lives in the roots of clover and pea plants, which helps the plants to obtain nitrogen from the soil. Growing such plants in soil which is poor in nitrogen helps to enrich it. Other types of bacteria help to turn milk into yoghurt. Many **herbivores** have bacteria inside their intestines which help them digest grass and other plant material. Some of these bacteria produce vitamins and proteins useful to the animal in which they live.

Viruses are microscopic organisms which are neither plants nor animals. They can be thought of as **parasites** of animal and plant cells. Viruses are almost crystal-like in appearance, with a tough outer coat. Their core is made of a chemical called **deoxyribonucleic acid**, or DNA. This chemical is found in all living things. Viruses cannot exist without the help of cells of other living organisms. When a virus meets a cell of the right kind, it bores into it and injects its DNA core into the cell. Once inside, the virus takes over the cell's chemistry and makes it produce copies of the virus. Eventually the cell dies and the new viruses escape to invade other cells.

Different viruses attack different organisms. Many plant diseases are caused by virus attacks. The infecting virus particles are injected into the plant by insects feeding on the plant. Virus diseases in humans include influenza, yellow fever and measles.

Biologists have difficulty in deciding whether bacteria and viruses are plants or animals. For example, some bacteria obtain energy from breaking down large molecules. This is something animals do. Others use simple raw materials in the same way as plants. Viruses are even more difficult to classify. Most biologists place bacteria and viruses in groups of their own.

Scientists have been able to learn more about life on the microscale in recent years. This is because they now have better microscopes to work with. A great advance was made with the development of the **electron microscope**. This instrument not only produces clearer pictures but it also gives much bigger magnifications of micro-organisms. More recently, the scanning electron microscope has produced even better results. This microscope allows the biologist to get a three-dimensional view of life on the microscale.

The cycles of life

ALL ANIMALS AND PLANTS die eventually and need to be replaced if their species is to survive. All organisms replace themselves by **reproduction**. The simplest way of reproducing is to split into halves. Each half becomes a new organism which grows before splitting again. Some of the most simple protozoa, such as amoebae, reproduce in this way. Inside every amoeba is a **nucleus**. This is the 'computer' of the cell, controlling its activity and growth.

The amoeba is one of the simplest living organisms. It is less than 0.5mm in size. Every few days it reproduces by dividing into two parts. The central part of the amoeba, called the nucleus, also divides at the same time.

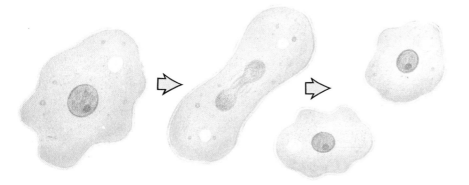

When the amoeba divides, the nucleus also splits into two. Each part becomes the nucleus of one of the new cells. This type of reproduction is called **asexual reproduction**. This means that the organism is producing copies of itself without the need for males and females.

Another example of asexual reproduction is found in an animal called a **hydra**. This very small organism lives in ditches and ponds. The hydra uses long tentacles to catch small plants and animals as food. When food is plentiful, the hydra produces tiny buds which grow into new hydra. Once large enough, these buds break away to begin life on their own as new hydra. Many plants are able to produce new plants by asexual reproduction. A cutting of a geranium, or a leaf of an African violet, will grow into another plant. Organisms created by asexual reproduction have one thing in common: they are exact copies of their parent.

When we look carefully at most plants and animals in the world, we can see that each individual differs from the next. Think of a litter of puppies, or even the members of your own family. Each puppy or person is different from the others. These differences, or variations, are the result of the mixing of features from the parents.

Nearly all organisms exist in two special forms which we call male and female. Male animals produce special reproductive cells called **sperms** and the male reproductive part of plants is called **pollen**. Females produce their own special cells called eggs. Each of these male and female cells is different from every other cell in the body of the plant or animal. Each contains only half of the material and information needed to create a new organism.

When each sperm, or pollen grain is joined to an egg cell, we call this **fertilization**. Once fertilization has occurred then the new organism can begin to grow. By bringing together these special cells from males and females, a new mixture of information is produced every time. This is why there is so much variation between puppies of a litter, or members of your family. This type of reproduction is called **sexual reproduction**.

Not all organisms have separate sexes. Animals such as earthworms, slugs and snails have

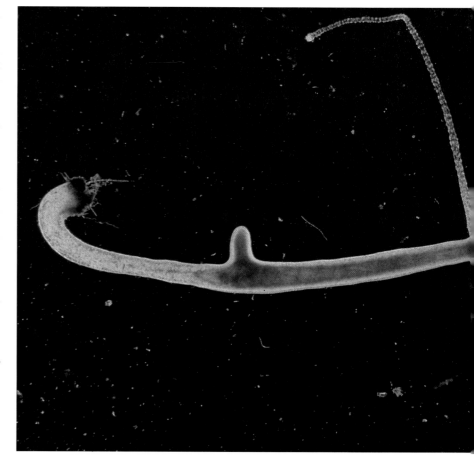

n the summer, large numbers of wingless nymphs, or young greenflies, are produced by the adult females. The eggs are not fertilized by the males. Once the summer has ended, sexual reproduction takes place to produce more young greenflies, and these do have wings.

The hydra *(below)* is found in fresh water ponds and ditches. It can grow to a length of 3cm. The tentacles are used for catching food and for movement. To the left of the tentacles you can see the bud. This will grow, and break away to form a new hydra.

both sexes in the same individual. Most plants also have male and female parts in one flower. Such organisms are called **hermaphrodites**. This does not mean that they can fertilize their own eggs with their own sperm or pollen. Snails exchange sperm and fertilize each other's eggs.

Most plants have flowers which carry both male and female parts. The 'eggs' of the plant are hidden away in an **ovary** at the base of the petals. The male sex cells, or pollen, are produced on long filaments, or **anthers**. Most plants avoid fertilizing themselves, by producing pollen and eggs at different times. The usual situation is that pollen appears, or is mature, first. This is picked up by visiting insects and carried to other flowers. Once all the pollen has gone, the ovaries will develop and produce a sticky tip, or **stigma**. Insects visiting the flower, to feed upon the sugary nectar, will leave behind pollen grains from another plant stuck to the stigma. The pollen reaches the egg, deep inside the ovary, by growing a long tube down into the ovary. Once the egg is reached, the information carried by the pollen grain then joins with that of the egg to start the formation of a seed.

These two ways of producing new organisms, called asexual and sexual reproduction, are used for different reasons. When food is plentiful and the weather is good, female greenflies produce young greenflies without the eggs being fertilized. This asexual reproduction in greenflies produces tiny copies of the female in great numbers. When winter approaches, the greenflies produce young with wings, both males and females. These winged greenflies mate, thus bringing together sperms and eggs. Their young, produced by sexual reproduction, are all slightly different from one another. Each is adapted to a slightly different situation and thus at least some will survive until summer when food is plentiful.

petal

stigma

anther

ovary

stamen

ovules

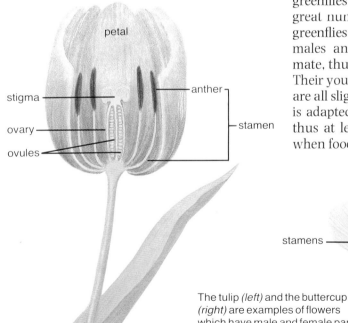

petal

stamens

ovary

The tulip *(left)* and the buttercup *(right)* are examples of flowers which have male and female parts within a single bloom. The ovules, or eggs, are developed in the ovary. The male parts of a flower are called stamens. At the tip of each stamen is the anther containing pollen.

Eggs and seeds

MOST ANIMALS produce eggs at the start of the life cycle. Eggs contain all the food and protection needed for the growth of a new animal. Most animals have separate male and female sexes. Only females produce eggs and these have to be fertilized by sperm cells from a male before growth begins. A bird's egg has all the features common to the eggs of other animals, and has other characteristics as well. It is like a space capsule, containing everything necessary to support life.

The orange-coloured yolk is the food store which is provided for the tiny, growing ball of cells, or **embryo**. This is the living part of the egg which develops into a new individual. The space between the yolk and shell of the egg is filled with a clear, sticky liquid called **albumen**. This helps to cushion the yolk and embryo against shocks. Another valuable purpose of the albumen is to keep the yolk from drying out or becoming infected with bacteria. The whole egg is enclosed inside a hard shell made from a web of protein and a chemical called **calcium carbonate**.

The shell protects the yolk and embryo from being crushed and is not as delicate as we are made to think. An egg shell has been shown to resist pressures equivalent to 1500 kg per square centimetre. The shell is full of micro-

scopic pores that allow oxygen to pass through into the egg. The oxygen which we take in when we breathe is essential to all living cells, and the embryo would quickly die without it.

Each part of a bird's egg is separated from the other parts by very thin layers of 'skin' called membranes. The yolk is surrounded by a tough **vitelline membrane**. This is drawn out on either side of the yolk into twisted strands attached to the ends of the shell. This membrane protects the yolk and keeps the developing embryo in the centre of the egg. Under the shell are two membranes which are there as barriers to bacteria. Without them the bacteria would eventually kill the embryo.

The eggs of many other animals are much simpler than those of birds. All have a developing embryo, a yolk and some form of shell.

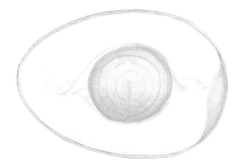

In the centre of the egg *(left)* is the yolk, containing its small embryo. The yolk is held in place by a skin-like membrane attached to the ends of the shell. On the right is the developing embryo which uses the yolk as food. If the egg is kept warm (incubated) by the mother bird, the chick will be ready to hatch after twenty-one days.

(right) The eggs, or spawn, of the salmon. Thousands of eggs are laid in the upper reaches of rivers. After two or three years in fresh water, the young fish swim down to the sea. There they grow into mature adults.

(right) The familiar sight of the dandelion head. Each seed is designed to be carried by the wind to a new place, where it can settle and grow into a new plant.

Cuckoos do not build their own nests. Instead, they lay eggs in the nests of other birds. In this case, the cuckoo has chosen to lay a single, larger egg in the nest of a twite, or mountain linnet.

A single egg of the brown hairstreak butterfly *(far right)*, greatly magnified.

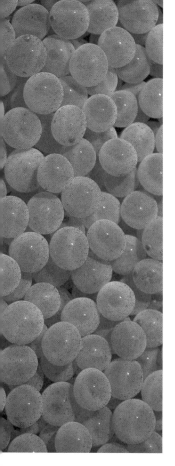

Among the most common egg-laying groups are the insects. Nearly all the million or so species of insects lay eggs. Their eggs are protected by a beautifully shaped shell, made from the same material as their outer skeleton, called **chitin**. Insect eggs contain only a little yolk and the newly hatched young are very small. Most insects lay large numbers of eggs. This is because many insects will be eaten or will die. The queen ant lays millions of eggs each year. Only a few of these survive to become adult ants.

Most fish also lay lots of small eggs in batches, called **spawn**. These eggs are fertilized in water by the male fish squirting a liquid, containing sperm, over the eggs. Frogs and toads also lay eggs in huge batches and rely upon a similar method of fertilization.

All animals need to lay a certain number of eggs in order to maintain their species, the number varying from one species to another. Small birds, such as the wren, need to lay twelve or so eggs at a time, and they may have two or more clutches in one year. Most of the young chicks will be eaten by other birds and animals. Large birds, such as eagles and some sea birds, lay one or two eggs only per year. They are better able to protect their eggs and young chicks. The protection of vulnerable eggs is taken to extremes by mammals such as humans, cows, dogs and cats.

The egg of the mammal is kept inside the female body in a special organ called a **uterus**. A mammal egg is very small compared to the size of the animal, as it contains almost no yolk. Fertilization occurs inside the female's body and the egg grows within the uterus or **womb**. The small embryo develops in a warm, safe environment and is provided with all the food it needs by the mother's blood system. The care of the young mammal continues after it has been born.

Plants produce eggs, called seeds after they have been fertilized. Like animal eggs, seeds have a tough outer coat and contain food for the embryos. Each seed contains only one embryo. Seeds are produced in very large numbers by some plants. This is to ensure that at least one or two manage to survive and grow into new plants. One major difference between a plant seed and an animal egg is that plant seeds have special shapes and structures that help them spread, or disperse. Plants tend to remain fixed in one position, while most animals can move around and place their eggs in the best places for development. Seeds may be adapted for dispersal by a number of means. Some, such as the coconut, are spread by the movement of water. Dandelion seeds are each provided with a 'parachute' to carry the seed on the wind. Teasels and some grasses have seeds covered in tiny hooks which cling to the coats of passing animals until they drop off. Pansy seed pods explode suddenly to scatter their seeds far and wide.

The essential point about all seeds and fertilized eggs is that they protect and feed the developing embryo. The variety in size and ways of surviving is enormous. Every plant or animal has developed its own way of facing the problem of survival. As in most things, variety helps to create the richness of life we see around us.

The bright orange rose hip attracts birds which eat the fruit. However the seeds are not digested, and are carried some distance before they pass out with the droppings of the bird.

Courtship and reproduction

ALL ANIMALS AND PLANTS live for only a certain length of time. This period of time is called their **life span**. If they are to keep their species in existence, all animals and plants must produce copies of themselves. The way they do this is called reproduction. Most plants and animals have two parts to their life span, a developing, or young stage, and an adult stage. As a plant grows from a tiny seed, energy is put into making leaves, roots and stems. A young animal, likewise, puts much of its effort into growing larger and more like its parents. An important change occurs when the plant or animal becomes adult, or mature. In a full-grown plant much of the energy goes into producing flowers, fruit and seeds. Many adult animals spend a large amount of energy producing young animals or laying eggs. Most female insects spend all their short lives producing eggs, which hatch into the next generation.

Reproduction includes all the activities that lead to production of seed or young animals. In many plants, this involves attracting suitable insects to bring pollen to fertilize the **ovule** in the flower. In animals, reproduction includes attracting or finding a partner, mating, and, for many animals, caring for the young. The most

The male ladybird *(left)* mates with the female, resting his legs on her back. Ladybirds are useful to us because they eat garden pests such as aphids.

The female salmon *(below)* lays her eggs in the bed of a river. These eggs are then fertilized by the male salmon.

vital part of reproduction is the joining together of special male cells called **spermatozoa** with egg cells produced by the female. In animals the action of placing spermatozoa near the egg, to allow fertilization to take place, is called mating, or **copulation**. The process of fertilization can take place inside the female's body, as in most animals, or outside, as with fishes and frogs.

The hoverfly plays its part in pollination. While feeding on nectar it becomes covered with the yellow pollen. This is then carried to another flower, and fertilization of the ovules in that flower takes place.

Before a female animal will allow a male animal to mate with her, she has to be satisfied that he is of the same species as herself. To be sure of this all animals go through a play-act, or **courtship** ritual. Courtship can take many forms depending upon the animals involved. An example of one type is the 'dance' between crested grebes. The female and her suitor will go through a series of movements and sounds which each bird instinctively knows. Colours are very important in such courtship displays. A general rule among animals is that the male is the more colourful and usually the one who approaches the female.

Sounds can play a very important part in courtship. The male grasshopper approaches his partner with a special 'tune' that she recognizes as an invitation to mating. If she has already mated and is only interested in laying her eggs, she will ignore him until he goes away. If she is ready for mating she will answer him with a special 'tune' of her own. Many insects and other animals court each other using scents called **pheromones**. Each animal has certain scents for alarm and others for persuading the female to mate.

In animals, such as deer, the females are attracted to the largest and most impressive males. Each autumn the deer collect in certain areas and males, or stags, have mock fights. The winners will then have the right to mate from females in the herd. This is called **rutting**. In a bird called the ruff, the males collect in open fields and set up small circles, or **leks**, where they show off their colourful plumage. The female ruff is attracted to one of the largest, most colourful males and moves into his space within the lek and lets him mate with her. In these last

During the breeding, or rutting season, the red deer stags have pushing contests, using their antlers. These mock battles are performed to impress females.

(1) Great crested grebes discover each other in this opening ceremony; (2) the head-shaking ceremony: they approach each other with heads lowered; (3) the retreat ceremony: one of the birds dashes away; (4) fish offering: the male gives a gift to his mate; (5) the penguin dance: they dive to collect weed, then rise up facing each other.

two examples a single male may mate with several females. The contests between males are harmless and they seldom hurt each other. This is nature's way of making sure that the best-adapted males can pass on their qualities to the next generation; this is sometimes called the survival of the fittest.

An important requirement for reproduction in many animals is having an area of ground called a **territory**. This is a living space for the family. In this space a male will defend, feed and bring up his family or **offspring**. The robin is a good example of a territorial bird. Each male chases off any intruding male from his territory. The red breast of the robin is his warning signal to other male robins. Small mice and shrews are also very territorial. The high-pitched squeaks that you may hear in fields are often disputes between males over the border between their territories. If mate-finding, courtship and mating have been successful, then some of the young animals which have been produced will grow up to reproduce and keep the species alive.

Life on six legs

To MOST PEOPLE, an insect is any small animal that flies or crawls. The way to tell a real insect is to count its legs. A true insect has six legs. Spiders, for example, are not insects because they have eight legs. The insects are by far the largest group of animals in the world. Over 750 000 different types, or species, have already been named. It has been estimated that a further 250 000 still wait to be discovered. One 'small' group of beetles has more species in it than all the species of birds, fish and mammals put together.

Insects are the most successful group of animals if judged by numbers and variety. They are found everywhere; on land, in fresh water, and even on the seashore. Some of the earliest animals to come on to land were probably insects. Large dragonflies, similar to those that fly around your local pond, were alive and thriving 345 million years ago. The secret of insect success lies in their hard outer covering called the cuticle. This is very strong and light, rather like fibreglass from which we make canoes. The insect cuticle has a very thin layer of wax on the outside to stop water passing through. Safe within their waterproof armour, insects have invaded everywhere you can imagine, from the driest deserts to the deepest lakes.

All insects are made up of three main parts: the head, a body, or **abdomen**, and a middle section called the **thorax**. The head carries all the important parts for survival, such as the eyes, mouth and brain. The abdomen holds the

digestive system and, if adult, the reproductive organs. The thorax is the engine of the insect, holding the huge muscles that power the legs and wings. The whole body of an insect is covered with minute sense organs. These tell the insect how warm or wet it is in the outside world or even what a certain plant tastes like. Most insects have one or two pairs of wings depending upon the species. Others, such as beetles, fold their wings away when not in use and hide them under a hard wing-case.

Like an armour-plated tank, the rhinoceros beetle *(above)* is well able to avoid being damaged. The shiny front wings cover most of the beetle's body. They also protect the hind wings which are smaller and more fragile.

The body of an insect is divided into three parts, head (right), thorax (centre) and abdomen (left). All insects have six legs, and most insects can fly.

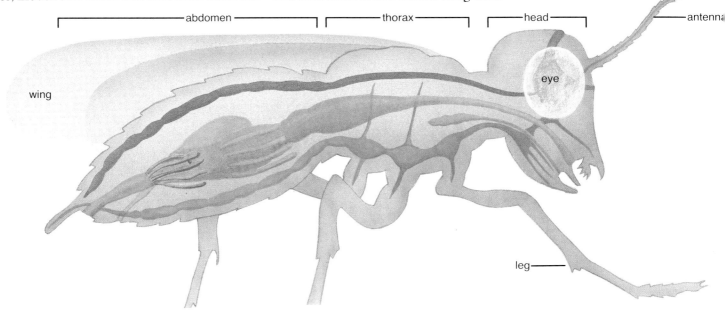

abdomen — thorax — head — antenna

wing

eye

leg

Insects can only increase their size by getting rid of their old cuticle and producing a new, larger one. All insects begin life as an egg. This hatches either into a tiny copy of the parent, called a **nymph**, or into a caterpillar, called a **larva**, which looks nothing like the parent. The grasshopper is a good example of an insect that produces a nymph. Each 'young' grasshopper goes through five or six changes of its outer cuticle or 'skin' before finally becoming a fully-winged, adult grasshopper. Butterflies lay eggs that hatch into caterpillars. These caterpillars go through four to six 'skin' changes before becoming a chrysalis or **pupa**. This strange animal has no legs or wings or, indeed, anything insect-like. The pupa is a mould in which

(right) Four stages in the metamorphosis of butterflies. The eggs, laid by the butterflies, turn into larvae (caterpillars). In time, each caterpillar becomes a pupa, or chrysalis. From this pupa emerges a new butterfly, and so on.

Dung beetles live and breed in animal dung and serve a useful purpose in the spreading and recycling of natural products. They are related to the scarab beetles which were worshipped by the ancient Egyptians.

the shape of the adult butterfly will be formed. The adult emerges from the pupa after a few weeks. Once an insect becomes an adult it does not grow any more. A small fly does not grow into a bigger fly.

Almost anything that can be used as food will be eaten by one insect or another. Every type of plant has its own special insect species which feeds upon it. Other plant-visiting insects like bees and butterflies help to pollinate fruit trees and other crops. The plant-eating insects are, themselves, food for yet more types of insect. For example, the ferocious tiger beetle or the praying mantis chase and eat other insects. All animals eventually die and there are insects waiting to eat the flesh, hair and sometimes even the bones of dead animals.

The peak of insect success is reached by the so-called **social insects**. Ants and termites form civilizations that rival those of human beings. Bees and wasps make their own world inside their nests, controlling both the temperature and the size. These insects are able to build organized societies by creating special worker and soldier classes. Inside each nest is a single queen who lays all the eggs and controls what workers do.

The huge variety and number of insects make them one of the most important groups in the whole animal and plant world. Perhaps we should be thankful that they are not any larger, otherwise the world would be a very different place.

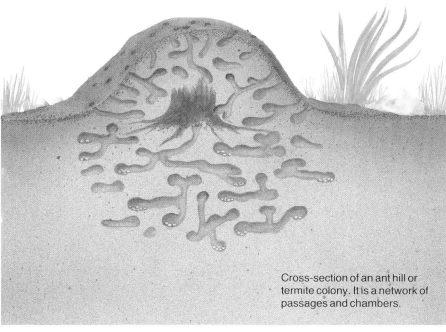

Cross-section of an ant hill or termite colony. It is a network of passages and chambers.

Predators

Animals which catch and eat other animals are called **predators**. Each region of the world has a variety of predators. The cold arctic wastes are the home of the polar bear, a fierce predator that eats seals and fish. It will also attack human beings. The hot, dry plains are the home of the lion. In the oceans are the sharks and some flesh-eating whales. These, too, are predators.

All these animals have very sharp teeth and powerful jaws. They catch and kill other animals by sheer power and strength. The animals that become food for predators are called **prey**. These may be harmless, plant-eating animals, **herbivores**, or other smaller predators. Very few animals would try to attack a lion or polar bear. The young lion and bear cubs are not quite so safe and may be eaten by other predators.

The main characteristic of all predators is their teeth, and in many species, sharp claws. Each type of predator has teeth adapted to the kind of prey it catches. Lions have long, pointed teeth with which they kill and tear their prey apart. The tiny, mice-like shrews have small, pointed teeth which they use to crack open and

The polar bear is one of the most dangerous of all animals. It feeds mostly on seals and fish, and is an excellent swimmer.

The white-headed sea eagle. It has a sharp, hooked beak, well designed for killing its prey and tearing flesh.

crush beetles. The eagle has a sharp, hooked beak to tear and pull away the flesh of a rabbit or other small animal.

Many insects have thin, pointed mouth parts with which they pierce and suck dry their prey. Some predators use stones or sticks to attack their prey. Sea otters break open clams against their bellies, using a stone. Chimpanzees poke insects out of cracks and crevices with sticks and grass stems. The most dangerous and cunning predator of all is the human. Since early times humans have been developing newer and better ways of catching and killing animals. With the development of weapons all animals were threatened by the hunters.

The predator's way of life is a difficult one. Most animals, with the exception of the top predators such as the lion and polar bear, are in constant danger of being eaten themselves. There are a number of natural ways by which animals can avoid being eaten by predators. Many animals are protected by camouflage or by containing poisons which make them unpleasant to eat.

The lion is camouflaged in the grassy plains of Africa, but for a different reason. The lion catches an antelope or zebra by creeping up on the unsuspecting animal until it is close enough to chase and catch it. Camouflage helps the lion to approach unseen. The cheetah catches its prey by sheer speed. These sleek, powerful animals can outrun the fastest antelope or gazelle. The wild dogs of Africa hunt in groups, or

animal over 30 m long, lives on small sea animals called **krill**. These are strained from the sea water by the specially adapted filter in the mouth of the whale.

Energy is one key to the way in which predators feed. A lion uses lots of energy to stalk, kill and eat a zebra. Once the lion has fed, it will sit around resting for several days. The blue whale uses very little energy in catching krill. These creatures are sieved out of the water as the whale swims along. The size of the prey must be large enough for it to be worthwhile for the predator to chase and eat it. We also have the choice of living on one good meal per day or nibbling constantly at nuts or cereals. We can obtain many of our daily needs from one good meal of meat and vegetables. On the other hand, we could spend all day eating individual pieces of breakfast cereal. These are the sorts of choices that have shaped the relationship between predators and their prey.

(above) Lions hunt and kill only when they are hungry. This may be once a week. At other times they roam and laze around, yawning from time to time like this one. Its sharp pointed teeth are clearly visible.

(left) The kingfisher dives into the stream to catch its prey. Its long beak, with serrated (toothlike) edges, is well adapted for gripping slippery fish.

The praying mantis is so called because it holds its legs in the attitude of prayer. It lies in wait for its victim, then, gripping it tightly, commences the meal.

The swiftest of all land animals, the cheetah *(below)*, relies on speed to overtake its prey. A cheetah can run over short distances at a speed of 120 kph.

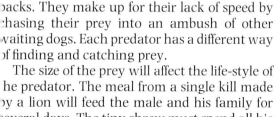

backs. They make up for their lack of speed by chasing their prey into an ambush of other waiting dogs. Each predator has a different way of finding and catching prey.

The size of the prey will affect the life-style of the predator. The meal from a single kill made by a lion will feed the male and his family for several days. The tiny shrew must spend all his waking hours catching and eating small insects, merely to stay alive. The larger the predator, the larger the prey and the less often it has to feed. There are exceptions, such as the anteater. These large animals feed by digging open ants' nests and using their sticky tongues to catch and eat them. The blue whale, a huge

Energy producers in the living world

ALL FORMS OF LIFE need energy in order to carry out their normal daily processes. They also need energy for growth and, in the case of most animals, for movement in the environment. Movement uses up large amounts of energy.

Energy exists in a number of forms and can be changed from one form to another. Heat and light are two different forms of energy. The Earth receives energy in the form of sunlight. Green plants use the light energy from the Sun to make food by the process of photosynthesis. During this process, the light energy is changed into **chemical energy**. This energy is stored in the chemical substances produced as a result of photosynthesis. These substances are sugars such as **glucose**. The sugars provide the basic energy from which all other foods are made. Thus green plants form the first link in any food chain. Herbivores get their energy from the plants they eat. Some of this energy is passed on to **carnivores** when the herbivores are themselves eaten.

We can use the energy of the Sun in a special way. Our power stations burn fossilized plants and organisms as coal or oil, releasing the energy locked into them by sunlight millions of years ago. We convert the stored chemical energy in these **fossil fuels** into electricity, which can then provide us with light and heat.

Animals and plants produce heat when they release energy from their food. Heat is therefore a common form of energy.

Some animals and plants produce other forms of energy. These are unusual but fascinating. For example, specialized animals and plants can produce their own light energy and some fish can even produce their own electricity. One of the best known light producers is an insect called the firefly. This can produce bursts of light from specially adapted parts of its body. These flashes are used to signal to other fireflies and are especially useful in attracting a mate. The glow-worm, which is a kind of beetle, is another light-producing insect. It produces a steady greenish light from an organ at the tip of its abdomen.

The special thing about firefly and glow-worm light is that it is produced by a chemical called **luciferin**. This is rather like the pigment chlorophyll in plants. However, instead of turning sunlight into food, it changes the chemical energy in food back into light. Unlike the light of electric bulbs and candles, the light of fireflies and glow-worms produces no heat. These small insects are able to do something we cannot do. They can produce light without wasting much of the energy as heat.

Many microscopic single-celled plants and animals, that live in lakes and the sea, glow in

(right) The neon tetra is so called because of the attractive, glowing stripe which runs from above the eye to the tail. This makes it very popular as an aquarium fish. The iridescence has its source in pigment cells. There are many species of 'glowing' tetra and they mostly come from Central and South America.

These Jersey cows are herbivores. They get their energy from the green plants that they eat. Some of this food energy is released as water vapour. During the process known as respiration, animals take in oxygen, giving off carbon dioxide and water vapour. The water vapour enters the atmosphere, eventually condensing into water droplets which return to the soil as rain.

Some animals produce electrical energy. The electric eel, which lives in the muddy waters of the Amazon River in Brazil, can produce quite powerful bursts of electricity, sometimes as high as 550 volts. The amount of electricity produced in a single burst by another fish, the electric ray, is sufficient to light twenty or more electric light bulbs. Such strong electric currents are used by these fish as a means of defence and also to stun or kill their prey. These currents are even large enough to kill a human. The electricity is produced by special parts of the fish's body which have been modified from muscle cells. They are stacked along the length of the body, rather like cells in an ordinary battery.

Many fish produce much lower currents which are often produced as bursts and used

the dark. This is called **bioluminescence**. Scientists do not understand how this happens but once again it involves the conversion of the chemical energy in food into light.

Almost all deep-sea fish have spots or patches that glow in very deep parts of the oceans which are completely dark. The deep-sea angler fish dangles a strange fleshy lobe in front of its mouth. The tip of this lobe glows and is thought to attract unsuspecting fish into the reach of the angler fish's waiting jaws.

Certain tropical fungi can also produce light. During the Second World War, soldiers fighting in the jungles in the Far East were able to make use of this fact. At night they carried branches on which these fungi were growing. The fungi glowed in the dark and the light they produced helped the soldiers to find their way on night patrol.

Fireflies *(right)* are beetles. The females have luminous organs which give out a greenish light. These organs are flashed as signals to attract the males.

The electric ray *(left)* can stun its enemies with an electric shock. The current produced would be strong enough to light twenty or more electric light bulbs.

The dogfish *(below)* uses weak electrical currents to detect fish hidden in the seabed.

rather like **radar**. These fish can pick up the returning signals and use them to help detect changes in their surroundings. The common dogfish can use weak electrical currents to detect small fish hidden in the sand. Some small river fishes use very rapid bursts of current, almost like radio waves, and may be able to communicate with each other.

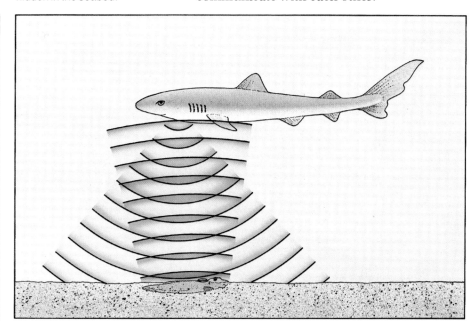

Flight in the living world

ANIMALS keep their feet on the ground because of gravity, a force that pulls them towards the centre of the Earth, allowing them to live on its surface. Gravity is a powerful but invisible force. Without it no person can stand or run, no snake can slide through the undergrowth and no river can flow to the sea. And yet, despite this, a surprising number of animals manage to travel through the air close to the Earth without disappearing into space. They do it by flying.

The albatross *(right)* is noted for its gliding flight. The bird can glide and soar for long periods, using the strong winds in the southern hemisphere. Some species of albatross have a wingspan of up to 3.5m. They are the widest-winged of all birds.

Although not capable of controlled flight, the leaping frog *(left)* is adapted to glide. Its webs and skin flaps outstretch as it launches itself into the air. They act like a kind of parachute, so that the frog can glide gently to another tree or to the ground.

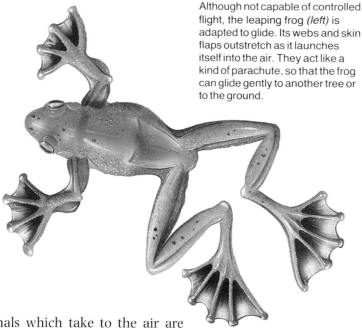

Not all animals which take to the air are capable of true, controlled flight. Some lizards and frogs, and even one species of snake in South East Asia, climb trees and then launch themselves into the air to escape their enemies or to reach the ground as quickly as possible. Some species have skin stretched between their fingers and toes or along their bodies, and they parachute gently down. They are actually pulled down by gravity, but the stretched skin acts as a brake against the air and they land without hurting themselves. Flying fish cannot really fly. They swim at high speed through the

The bee *(below)* has two pairs of wings which are connected in flight. The wings move very rapidly in a figure-eight pattern. This gives more lift and thrust on the down beat, at the same time twisting to reduce air resistance. The wings are powered by the thorax, to which they are connected by two sets of muscles. The up beat is controlled by one set and the down beat by the other.

water and then break the surface to launch themselves into the air above. Then they spread their body fins wide and sail as much as 400 m through the air.

The true fliers of the animal kingdom are found among the insects, the birds and, alone among mammals, the bats. They all have powerful body muscles. These supply the energy to drive their wings with enough power to keep them off the ground. Once airborne, they can twist, turn and dive with skill and speed. Some of them can even make journeys of several thousand kilometres.

The bat *(left)* is the only mammal with controlled flight. Each wing is formed from a sheet of skin stretched over a frame of arm and finger bones.

(above) In fast forward flight, the bird's wings are pulled downwards and forwards by strong muscles. During the downstroke, the wing tip rotates, and this drives the bird forwards. On the recovery stroke the wing bends, and the shoulder rotates to bring the wing up again for the next downstroke.

beats its wings downwards, it moves forward because the feathers are forced against the air. At the same time, the air is forced backwards. The upward stroke of the wing is less powerful and the feathers are opened more to let air through. In this way the whole bird is moved forward. The curve of the wing traps air underneath and holds the bird up, even though the force of gravity is trying to pull it down.

Different birds have differently shaped wings to suit their needs. The most remarkable is the hummingbird, which twists its wings on the upward stroke so that the effect is the same as on the downward stroke. In this way, beating its wings about seventy times each second, it can hover, or remain still in the air, as it feeds on the nectar of plants.

Insects were the first animals to fly properly. They did this nearly 300 million years ago. Small flaps on their bodies would have allowed them to glide at first, but as these became larger, insects became better at flying.

Butterflies have four large wings, which they flap jerkily. These wings are unprotected and soon get torn, so the adult cannot fly for very long. It is important, then, that female butterflies find a mate and lay their eggs quickly.

Beetles have one pair of wings for flying, so they are not so good in the air as butterflies. But they have a second pair which have become hard and shiny. They can fold up their flying wings and hide them safely under these special wing-cases. This protection means that beetles can crawl over the ground without damaging their wings. A butterfly could never do this for long.

Flies have two small wings for flying. Close to this pair of flying wings, a second smaller pair is used to balance the fly in the air.

About 150 million years ago, insects were joined in the sky by the birds. Birds are the masters of flight. Their feathers and bones are strong and light, and even though feathers wear out, they are replaced each year, sometimes two or three times. When a bird in the air

The fast-beating wings of the tiny hummingbird *(right)* enable it to hover while it feeds on insects and nectar.

Trappers and engineers

ALL ANIMALS which feed on other animals face the problem of how to catch their food. Many animals search for and chase their prey, while others sit and wait for an unwary passing animal. A common way of catching food without too much effort is to build a trap or web. Spiders are the best example of animals that build webs to trap smaller animals for food. Their sticky webs are so fine as to be almost invisible. A passing insect does not see the trap until it is caught in the sticky threads. All that remains for the spider to do is to walk over the web and wrap up its tiny parcel of food, often to be kept as a meal for later. The spider is able to walk on the sticky web without being caught, because of oil on its feet.

Many other animals use nets to catch their food. The larvae of the small moth-like insects called **caddis-flies** live in streams, and some species spin nets between stones. These nets trap small animals washed downstream by the current. This is the same method as is used by salmon fishermen in river mouths.

Many strange organisms are found on the sea bed. Among them is a worm which casts out long, sticky threads. These are drawn in again and eaten, together with small animals and plants attached to the threads. Many organisms

The spider traps its prey in a silken, sticky web, so fine that it is almost invisible to unwary flies. Having netted the victim, the spider then wraps it up in a neat 'parcel' for future use.

The spiny-edged leaves of the Venus' flytrap *(above)* are like the jaws of an animal. When an insect touches the hairs in the centre of the trap, the leaves snap shut, trapping the prey. It is then dissolved by enzymes, and absorbed by the plant as food.

Corals and sponges on the seabed feed by sucking in seawater and filtering out all the microscopic animals and plants.

which are fixed to rocks or the seabed suck in sea water and filter out all the microscopic animals and plants. This method of feeding is carried out by corals and sponges. It is called filter feeding.

Some of the most interesting trappers are those plants which catch insects for food. The Venus' flytrap has large, spiny-edged leaves which can quickly fold over to enclose a fly or beetle. The strange pitcher plant has tall, tube-like leaves. In the bottom of each tube is a pool of liquid. Any flies or other small insects that wander on to the edge of the pitcher plant leaf slip down the smooth inner walls into the pool. Once caught there is no escape. The pool contains **enzymes** which kill each insect and break down its body. These plants have adapted to feed on insects because they live in places lacking in nitrogen, an element vital to life that is supplied by the bodies of insects.

We can compare human engineering and building with that of animals and plants. Cars are built with their strength in an outer shell, like many insects, crabs and spiders. Tall buildings are supported by strong pillars and deep foundations, like the trunk and roots of a tree. Other buildings are supported by steel frames, in the same way that the bones make up the skeleton of fishes, amphibians, reptiles, birds and mammals.

Examples of animal builders are numerous.

Beavers dam rivers and streams to create a lake of still water. In this they build their shelter, or lodge, out of tree branches. The entrances are always under water but the beavers' living area is above the water-line.

The nest of the weaver bird *(left)* is a fine construction of grass and leaves. It forms a safe environment for the eggs and growing chicks. The entrance to the nest is long and tubular to keep out predators.

Only a few millimetres long, each termite plays its part in building huge mounds of mud and earth. This is home for millions of termites and may last for a hundred years or more. A large mound may be 5 or 6 m high and 15 m around the base. Each mound contains a complicated network of tunnels and chambers where the members of the colony live.

The trappers and engineers of the living world can show us much about building and catching food. Seldom do we find an example of our own building methods that has not been used in a more simple form by some plant or animal.

The nests of birds are beautifully made to protect the eggs and, later, the growing chicks, and keep them warm. Each bird species uses different materials. The mud nest of the flamingo is totally different from the ball of feathers that makes up the goldcrest's nest. The oven bird of South America builds a large dome-shaped nest from mud. The nest has a hidden entrance so that the eggs are protected from predators. The shape of the nest gives the bird its name.

Animal builders can go to great lengths to make solid homes. The North American beavers build huge dams across small streams to create lakes in which an island shelter can be made. This house, or **lodge**, has an underwater entrance to keep out hungry wolves and bears. At the other end of the scale is the small termite.

Termites build huge mounds of mud and earth. Inside are complex systems of chambers and tunnels. Each mound is inhabited by millions of these tiny, ant-like insects.

Poisonous plants and animals

ONE OF THE MANY problems facing plants and animals is the danger of being eaten. Some animals are able to camouflage themselves, while others hide away. Some can fly and others can outrun their predators. Since plants cannot move, many of them are protected by sharp spines, hairs, or tough skins. Another way plants, and indeed many animals, are protected against predators is by the poisons they contain. These substances may not kill. However, they discourage other organisms from eating the plants and animals which produce them. Even animals which resemble those that produce poisons are protected from being eaten.

Plant poisons are among the most dangerous substances we know. The deadly poison **curare** is found in the bark of certain South American trees. Another powerful poison, found in the seeds of some tropical plants, is **strychnine**. Many colourful plants of the countryside contain poisons which make animals avoid eating them. For example, the bright yellow tree called **laburnum**, which grows in many European towns and cities, has poisonous seeds. Even the clover we find on lawns and meadows has a variety containing the poisonous chemical **cyanide** in its leaves.

Many plants have colourful flowers, some of which may be poisonous. In the animal world, however, the most colourful species are often the ones containing poisons. Nature has its own code of colours which warn others of danger. Bright reds, yellows and black often appear as bold markings on animals which are telling others to keep away. Once a bird has tasted the caterpillar of a cinnabar moth, in its black and yellow banded skin, that bird will, in the future, avoid all other animals with similar markings. The cinnabar caterpillar contains a poison which tastes so unpleasant that birds are im-

The caterpillar of the five-spot burnet moth *(right).*

The five-spot burnet moth *(below).* Both the caterpillar and the moth contain the poison cyanide. They are avoided by birds for this reason.

The giant hogweed *(left)* has flower stalks fanning out from the stem. It is extremely poisonous.

mediately sick if they eat it. The beautifully coloured burnet moths, in their deep blue and red patterns, look like butterflies, and fly in the daytime. They can do this without being in danger of attack by birds because they contain cyanide. This poison is picked up by their caterpillars as they feed on the clover species mentioned earlier. The caterpillar has evolved a method of storing the poison in such a way that it can be used to protect the adult moth. This method of protection is used by many butterflies and moths all over the world.

There are many unusual animals living in tropical parts of the world and some of these are poisonous. For example, there are numerous colourful frogs, toads and salamanders which gain protection from their poisonous skins. These poisons are often highly **toxic**. The golden arrow poison frog from South America con-

A desert scorpion killing a grasshopper, before eating it.

The black mamba *(left)* is the largest poisonous snake in Africa. It can grow to a length of 3m.

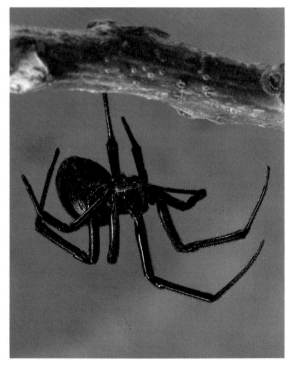

The black widow spider. Its powerful venom causes acute pain and paralysis. It can be fatal to children. Various black widow species are common in the southern United States. Since they are rather small they easily pass unnoticed, and this makes them all the more dangerous.

tains enough poison to kill more than two thousand adult humans.

Bright colours can also warn others that an animal has a poisonous bite or sting. The gaudy coral snakes of South America are banded black, red and yellow. They live without fear of being attacked because other animals recognize such colours as a warning. Those that ignore this seldom live for long. One of the most widespread warning patterns is that used by wasps, the bold black and yellow bands meaning 'keep your distance'.

Unlike the brightly coloured animals that contain poisons, some animals, using poisonous bites to kill their prey do not want to be seen. Instead, some hide in the shadows, and others are camouflaged. Scorpions, though small, can be very venomous. During the daytime they shun sunlight, hiding under rocks and in holes, but after dark they roam far and wide, searching for their prey.

Some of the most deadly creatures known to man are certain spiders. Their poison, or **venom**, is very difficult to deal with, even with modern medicines. The Australian funnel-web spider kills many people every year. Many poisonous snakes, however, are now less dangerous because of the use of modern drugs or **antidotes**.

Even the warm seas of the coral reefs are not safe, because of the deadly scorpion fish and weaver fish, with sharp spines that can pierce and poison the foot or hand of a careless bather.

Close relationships

MOST ANIMALS AND PLANTS live alone or within groups of their own species. Such organisms obtain all their food needs from their surroundings. Some animals and plants live with a species from another group. The hermit crab lives inside an old **mollusc** shell. Often there is a sea anemone attached to the outside of the shell. As the crab outgrows the shell it changes house into a bigger shell. After moving house, the crab usually moves the sea anemone as well. This type of relationship is of some value to the sea anemone which is given a firm base on which to live. The crab feeds on pieces of dead fish, and small pieces will float up and provide

The clown fish lives in the shelter of the sea anemone's tentacles, where it is safe from predators. Its bright yellow acts as a warning to enemies. This helps to protect the sea anemone as well as the clown fish.

some food for the sea anemone. In return the crab gains some protection because of the stinging tentacles of the sea anemone. This is a very simple type of relationship which is of benefit to both the crab and the sea anemone. However, either one can survive quite well without the other.

When two organisms live closely together and both gain something from the relationship, it is called **symbiosis**. Perhaps the best example of true symbiosis is shown by organisms called **lichens**. These very simple plants grow on rocks and tree trunks. The main body of the lichen is made from a type of **fungus**. On its own the

Lichens are simple plants consisting of fungus and algae living together. The fungus protects the algae from drying out and dying. The algae make food which supports the fungus.

fungus cannot survive. Within the fungal threads live tiny, single-celled plants called algae. These contain the pigment chlorophyll, which traps the energy of sunlight to make food. The algae produce sugars which the fungus can use as food. In return, the fungus protects the algae from drying out and dying. In this example of symbiosis the fungus gets food and the algae are protected, and so both benefit. This relationship differs from that of the hermit crab and sea anemone as neither fungus nor algae can live alone. There are many other examples of symbiosis in the living world, each differing in the way in which each partner benefits.

Not all close relationships work to the advantage of both partners. All animals and plants are attacked by parasites. This is the name given to organisms which obtain food

from some other animal or plant and give nothing in return. The animal or plant providing the food is called the **host**.

Humans are host to an enormous variety of parasites. Among the best known are tapeworms, round worms and insects such as lice and fleas. Tapeworms are long, ribbon-like animals which can live attached inside our intestines. They are **endoparasites**. Scientists once thought that tapeworms were entirely harmful and used up much of our food. It is true that large numbers of tapeworms can weaken the body and make it much more likely to become diseased. However, some scientists have shown that small numbers of tapeworms do no real harm and may even do some good by providing us with **vitamins**.

Round worms, or **nematodes**, are small, white worms with tough bodies. The parasitic nematodes attack all groups of plants and animals, taking food from them and giving nothing in return. In large numbers, they may even kill some animals and plants. Fleas and lice are called **ectoparasites** because they live on the outside of our bodies. These insects have sharp, needle-like mouth parts with which they can suck blood.

The blood of mammals, such as man, is a very convenient place to live for microscopic, single-celled parasites. This is because blood is full of food, nutrients and oxygen. All these materials are essential to the growth of viruses and para-

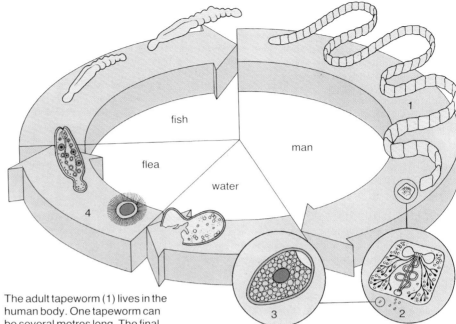

The adult tapeworm (1) lives in the human body. One tapeworm can be several metres long. The final segments (2, enlarged) separate, and eggs (3) from these are laid in the human faeces. The eggs hatch into larvae (4), and are eaten by water fleas. These, in turn, are eaten by fish, and secondary larvae are formed. If man eats the fish uncooked, the cycle may start all over again.

sitic protozoa. The close relationship between the host and the blood parasites is very one-sided. The parasite is able to grow and multiply very quickly. The host suffers from fevers and may even die. One of the most damaging blood parasites is the tiny protozoan that causes **malaria**. This protozoan, called *plasmodium*, lives for a time in the stomach of the mosquito. The parasite is passed from mosquito to human as the female mosquito feeds on blood. Once in the human bloodstream, the protozoa repro-

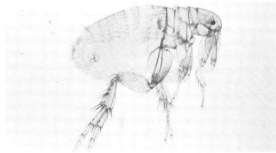

Fleas, known as ectoparasites, live on the host's exterior. The species of flea shown above lives on rats. Such fleas can transmit bubonic plague (black death) to humans.

The cleaner fish, seen inside the open jaws of a larger fish *(left)*. The cleaner provides a useful service by removing parasites from inside the mouth of its larger customer.

duce themselves and feed on blood and liver cells. In doing so they gradually kill the cells.

In the living world it is often difficult to recognize some close relationships. Scientists are still realizing how important symbiosis is to many plants. Perhaps one day the farmer will need to turn to such close relationships to increase crop yields.

Camouflage and mimicry

FEW ANIMALS, apart from humans, die of old age. Most end their lives as a meal for some other animal. Some animals avoid being eaten by running, flying or swimming away from danger. Others avoid predators by blending into the background which makes them difficult to see. This method of hiding is called **camouflage**. Many ground-feeding birds, such as grouse or woodcock, have mottled brown and cream feathers which help them to hide amongst the dead leaves and plants. Many insects, such as moths, are almost impossible to detect at rest on tree trunks or rocks. One such moth is the green carpet moth, which is perfectly camouflaged on trees or rocks covered in lichen, a type of plant.

When removed from their natural surroundings, many animals seem to be coloured very brightly, which you would think would make them easy to see. The black and orange of the tiger are very striking. In the forests of India, however, the tiger blends into the background. The bold stripes help to break up the outline of the animal and merge into deep shadow and bright sunspots. The cheetah spends much of its day sitting under trees on the East African

A green carpet moth at rest on a lichen-covered rock.

Flatfish, such as this plaice *(below)*, spend a lot of time on the seabed. Some change their colouring to match the sand, gravel, pebbles or stones on which they lie. Others can even vary the spots on their backs.

A nightjar sits motionless on the ground, relying on camouflage to protect it from predators. The varied colouring of the feathers blend with the leaf litter around it with such effectiveness that the bird's outline is very hard to see.

savannah. The dappled patches of sunspots and shade are perfect places to hide for the cheetah with its yellow and black patterned coat. The bold black and white stripes of the zebra are thought by some people to help camouflage it. These stripes may help to break up the outline of the zebra in what is called **disruptive camouflage.**

Some animals use camouflage to help them catch their food. One species of praying mantis in Malaysia is bright pink in colour. This strange colour helps it to sit unnoticed on flowerheads of pink orchids. Any unsuspecting flies that land on the orchid are quickly caught by the mantis and eaten. The chameleon is perhaps the most well known camouflaged hunter. These medium-sized lizards can be green or brown depending upon their background. If a green chameleon finds itself on a brown tree branch it can change the colour of its body to brown. Slow movements and matching camouflage help the chameleon to creep up on an insect. Once it is close enough, a long, sticky tongue does the rest. Some sea fishes, such as the plaice, are able to change their colour to match their background.

Throughout the living world, bright yellows, reds and black often mean danger. Many animals or plants with such colours may be poisonous or have painful bites or stings. Some animals have gained protection by copying these dangerous or inedible creatures. This special type of camouflage called **mimicry** relates to harmless animals, coloured or shaped like dangerous animals. The harmless animal, or **mimic**, need not be an exact copy of the dangerous animal. Enough protection is gained if the mimic can confuse a bird or other predator for only a few seconds. Such a delay is usually sufficient to allow the mimic to escape the predator by running or flying away. Many insects are protected in this way by mimicking bees and wasps. Hoverflies are often boldly striped black and yellow, but are completely harmless. Others are hairy and brown, just like honey bees or bumble bees. The wasp beetle

A branch with thorns, we might first assume. However, a closer look reveals a number of thorn bugs, which together produce a convincing illusion.

The crab spider *(below)* crouches almost invisibly in the centre of a marigold bloom. It is waiting to pounce on the first unsuspecting insect that is attracted to the flower.

could be mistaken for a real wasp, as it feeds on a flower. Even some moths have a wasp-like pattern.

When an edible, or harmless animal mimics a dangerous or poisonous one, this is called Batesian mimicry. This name comes from a biologist named Henry Bates, who first observed this protective colouring in the rain forests of South America. Also in the same forests, another biologist, Fritz Muller, noticed that many different kinds of butterfly all had a similar colour pattern. All the species involved were protected by one type of poison or another. If a bird tried to eat any of these butterflies the nasty taste would make it sick. Since the bird soon learns to avoid eating nasty insects by associating a pattern with the taste, all these different species of butterfly developed the same pattern. Once the common pattern has evolved, then all the butterflies or other animals that look alike are protected. This is called Mullerian mimicry. A familiar example is the yellow and black pattern of most wasps and hornets.

The variety and range of camouflage and mimicry is very great. Throughout the animal world the colour and shape of the individual have developed throughout millions of years of evolution. Thus each pattern and shape gives that particular animal the best possible chance of survival.

Rhythms and clocks

IF YOU WERE ABLE to visit the coral reefs of the southern Pacific at dawn on the day of the last quarter of the October–November moon, you would see an amazing sight. For a short time, the surface of the sea would look like a milky, writhing fluid. You would be witnessing the **spawning** behaviour of the palolo worm. Had you arrived at the same coral reef a day before, or a day after, you would have seen nothing unusual. The palolo worm spawns once a year, always on the same day and this never varies.

The giant leathery turtle behaves in a similar way. Between June and August every year,

The night and day rhythm is reversed in many cacti which live in sun-scorched regions. In order to preserve as much water as possible their stomata (the cells through which plants breathe) remain closed during the day to reduce evaporation to a minimum. Unlike other plants, cacti exchange carbon dioxide for oxygen at night.

Humans also show circadian rhythms. Our pattern of **urination**, for example, seems to follow a rhythm through a twenty-four-hour period. This, of course, can change depending upon our drinking habits. These rhythmic activities continue even when people no longer experience night and day. For example, rhythmic behaviour has been observed in astronauts orbiting the Earth.

Many patterns of rhythmic or **cyclic** behaviour are probably controlled by night and day. Frogs croak mainly at night, and the cockerel crows at or near dawn. However, many rhythms continue even when the environment is made constant as in a laboratory experiment. A scientist, Karl Hamner, carried out an interesting investigation. He took a

most of the world's female population of this turtle gathers on Trengaunu Beaches on the coast of Malaysia. Here they lay their eggs and then, afterwards, crawl back into the Pacific Ocean. Local people have learned to take advantage of this **rhythmic** behaviour. They wait for the turtles to finish laying and then take the eggs to sell them in the local markets.

Many organisms behave in a rhythmic way although not quite so dramatically as the palolo worm or the leathery turtle. For example, most animals become active at a particular time every twenty-four hours. Bats and owls fly and feed mainly at night. Many plants hold their leaves or flowers in one position at night and in another during the day. Plant **stomata** open and close following a daily rhythm. These daily rhythms of behaviour are called **circadian** or twenty-four-hour rhythms.

The giant leatherback turtle (above) can grow to over 2m in length and weigh 600kg. Although these turtles can be found in any tropical ocean, their nesting-beaches are restricted to two places, on the east coast of Malaysia and in Surinam in South America.

An eighteenth-century botanist, Carl Linnaeus, grew a floral clock in which the regular opening and closing of different flowers through the day marked the hours. This old postcard (right) shows how this can be done.

variety of animals and plants to the South Pole. There he placed them on a turntable which revolved at the same speed as the Earth. However, the turntable revolved in the opposite direction. In this experiment the animals were 'standing still' in space. There was no indication of daily time. All Hamner's experimental organisms still showed their circadian rhythms.

Other rhythmic activities seem to be related to phases of the Moon and to the rise and fall of the tides. Certain fiddler crabs change their colour and rate of activity between high and low tides. Crabs come out of their burrows at low tide to feed. At high tide they go back into their holes. Laboratory tests have shown that this pattern of behaviour continues even when the effect of the tides has been removed.

Many plants show cyclic patterns of behaviour which relate to seasonal changes of shorter days and colder temperatures. In temperate countries the leaves of **deciduous** trees change colour in autumn and fall off at the beginning of winter. Certain trees in tropical countries behave similarly. Here, however, the change is in response to rainy and dry seasons.

Many animals also have a seasonal rhythm of activity. For example, breeding often takes place in early spring so that the young develop and grow when there is plenty of food available in the late spring and summer. In the colder regions of the world, some mammals **hibernate** during the winter. This is another behavioural rhythm related to seasonal changes. Amphibians and reptiles behave in a similar way. Certain birds **migrate** twice each year and always at about the same time. By doing this, these animals are able to carry on the two basic activities of feeding and breeding.

The fiddler crab is only active at low tide. Scientists have found that it has its own biological clock which allows it to measure tidal time. Each low tide follows about twelve and a half hours after the previous one, a rhythm that the crab follows.

Organisms which continue to behave rhythmically even when placed in a constant environment must have some way of telling the time. Scientists now think that these animals have some kind of internal 'clock'. They call this mechanism a **'biological clock'**. We are not sure yet how these clocks work, but some scientists think that certain chemicals called **hormones** play an important part.

Sometimes biological clocks can be altered by changes in the environment. Travellers going from east to west or west to east on international jet flights often have difficulty in re-adjusting to the new situation in which they find themselves. Their own internal clocks get out of time with local conditions and we say they are suffering from **'jet lag'**. After a few days these people seem to adjust. The environment appears to be able to 'reset the clock'.

Passengers flying from London to New York pass through five hourly time zones. This means that on arrival after a flight lasting six hours forty minutes, they are five hours ahead of New York time. This confuses the human biological clock, which can take several days to adjust to the new local time.

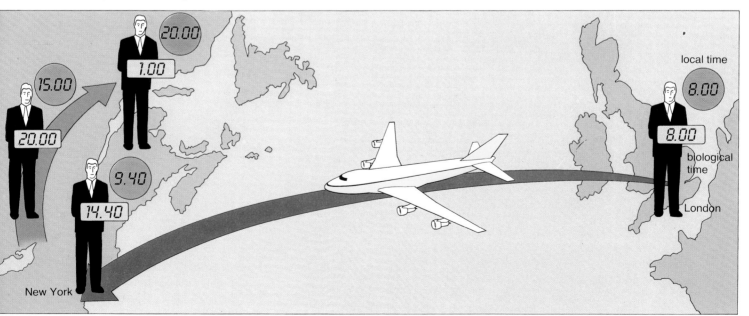

Migration and navigation

THE WORD **migration** is used to describe the movement of animals over large distances. Animals make these long journeys to change their habitat, for a variety of reasons. This may be because the area in which they live is overcrowded, or because their food supply may have run out. Many species move from one part of the world to another when the seasons change. Each year, as winter approaches, animals such as **caribou** migrate south to avoid the harsh weather and to find better feeding-grounds. This sort of migration happens every year at the same time, and generations of animals have learned the best routes to follow, crossing mountains and wading through rivers.

Every winter in Europe, huge flocks of birds fly to mudflats on the coasts, in order to feed upon worms and shellfish. For the rest of the year, these birds move inland to breed and bring up their young.

The record for the longest journey belongs to

During the summer, the Alaskan caribou feed on the small plants and shrubs of the tundra. In September the ground becomes barren and the southward migration begins. The caribou move in great herds away from the frozen world, taking their young with them. They have to travel 1000 km or more to reach the shelter and food supply of the northern forests.

The arctic tern holds the migration record. It breeds in the Arctic, flying southwards to winter in the Antarctic, not far from the South Pole. At one point, this bird has to fly 3000 km across the Antarctic Ocean without any land to guide it. In May the arctic terns fly northwards to their Arctic breeding grounds, covering on the round trip a distance of 18 000 km.

a bird called the arctic tern. Each year this fragile-looking bird flies from the Antarctic to regions in or near the Arctic in order to breed. Each year the adult birds fly 9000 km or so to the North, and return with their offspring in autumn, a round journey of about 18 000 km. Their ability to fly allows many breeds of birds to escape the cold, hard winters of northern continents. In spring, they return to rear a family on the plentiful harvest of insects or seeds. Swallows, swifts and storks are all among the many birds which leave Europe each autumn to winter in northern Africa. The snow goose breeds in Siberia, Alaska and Canada, wintering in western USA, especially California.

The fishes form another group of animals which migrate. The common eel, found in many streams and rivers in Europe, migrates more than 4800 km to breed. When they

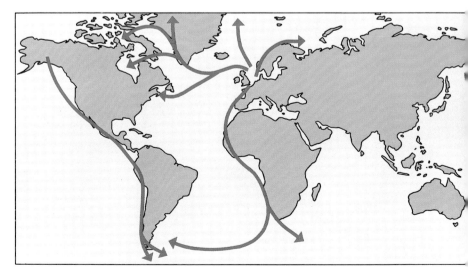

Salmon leaping Brook's river waterfall in Alaska. These fish battle their way upstream to spawn, sometimes leaping a fall of up to 3m in height.

A herd of migrating zebra, seen from the air. These grass-eating animals migrate, often with wildebeest and gazelle, to find better feeding grounds when the seasons change. On the way, they are attacked by predators.

and move up rivers in late autumn towards the same gravel beds and streams in which they were raised. The eggs, or **spawn**, are laid in shallow water, in among gravel, and the young hatch and grow in fresh water for two to three years before moving back into the sea.

Many animals migrate as their numbers increase and food runs out. The **lemming** is a small mouse-like creature which lives in northern Europe. Every five years or so they swarm in huge numbers, and seek out new feeding-grounds. In doing so, some do not stop once the sea is reached, and they drown trying to swim across it.

Some insects are regular migrating animals in many parts of the world. The North American monarch butterfly flies north in spring, and south in autumn. Locusts in Africa often descend upon crops after flying in huge swarms from their breeding-grounds where food has become scarce.

How do all these animals know which way to go? This is a question that has puzzled scientists. Some birds are thought to be able to tell where they are, or **navigate**, with the help of the position of stars. Another idea is that they use the **magnetic field** of the Earth as a guide. Migrating fish may use scents or chemicals in the water to guide them back to the stream in which they were born. For the most part, we are still puzzled as to how animals can tell north from south and east from west. One thing is clear: they do navigate very accurately. When you see birds on a telephone line in autumn, think of the long journey they are about to make. Yet those same birds may return to the same nest year after year. How they do so is an unsolved mystery.

become adult, the eels wriggle their way down rivers to swim across the Atlantic ocean. They head for a part of the ocean called the Sargasso Sea and here lay their eggs among its floating seaweed. The tiny young that hatch from the eggs do not look like eels, but are flattened and transparent. These small organisms drift and swim across the Atlantic, back towards Europe, aided by a sea current called the **Gulf Stream**. The journey may take two years and, during this time, they gradually take on the shape of an eel to become **elvers**. When they reach the coast of Europe, the elvers swim up the rivers to spend the next six years or so in small pools, streams and lakes.

Another long-distance traveller is the salmon. In this case, however, its migration is in the opposite direction to that of the eel. Some adult salmon live in the northern Atlantic Ocean, feeding and growing in the rich waters off Iceland. The fully grown salmon leave the sea

Hibernation

ANIMALS AND PLANTS which live in cold and temperate regions of the world face the problem of survival during the winter months. Many plants overwinter, or pass the winter, as seeds which germinate to produce new plants when spring arrives. Others die back and only the underground parts survive to grow when the temperatures become warmer. Many shrubs and trees lose their leaves as winter approaches and this is an adaptation to overwintering. New leaves emerge at the end of winter when the surrounding temperature increases.

All plant life adapts to cold, winter conditions in one way or another. Deciduous trees lose their leaves, and sprout new leaves in the spring. Under the snow, the grass dies back, and grows again at the beginning of spring.

Animals are more active organisms than plants and, because of this, they use more energy in carrying out their every day activities. Many animals are able to survive the winter without changing their behaviour. Others, however, take special precautions to avoid being killed by the cold.

Many single-celled animals pass the winter at the bottom of ponds and lakes. As winter approaches, a hard, protective **cyst** forms around each organism and it is then able to survive within this until the spring. Many insects pass the winter in the chrysalis stage, although some adult butterflies are able to survive cold temperatures if they can find a good place to hide.

The bullfrog *(right)* has been uncovered in its hibernating chamber. During the winter months, it lies 20 cm beneath the soil, returning to the surface at the end of winter.

Larger animals survive winter using other means. Some birds avoid the problem altogether and migrate to warmer lands. However the majority of animals stay where they are and overwinter in different ways. Fish, amphibians and reptiles are cold-blooded. Their blood temperature depends on the temperature of their surroundings. In warm conditions, the blood temperature is high but drops as the surroundings become colder.

At temperatures lower than 0°C, the blood of these animals would freeze. In order to avoid this, 'cold-blooded' animals have to hide away during the winter months. During this time they are in a state of **torpor**, which means they are very inactive. Amphibians and fish spend the winter at the bottom of ponds and lakes. Here, ice is less likely to form if conditions at the surface start to freeze. Reptiles shelter under-

ground, beneath stones and rocks, and in holes in tree trunks. Cold-blooded animals do not need to feed in winter. This is because they use very little energy while they are so inactive.

Mammals and birds are warm-blooded. Even in cold conditions their body temperature remains high. Despite this, some mammals find it difficult to live through the winter in the normal way. Bears, badgers and squirrels become very drowsy as winter approaches. They find a good place to shelter from the cold winds and then go to sleep. However, they do not sleep all winter and they wake up from time to time to feed on stored food.

Small mammals are very active in normal

40

conditions and their bodies use large amounts of energy. These animals are said to have a high **metabolic rate**. In order to maintain this and to keep warm, small mammals need to eat large amounts of food. However, food is often hard to find in winter. Many small mammals give up the struggle to remain active and keep warm, and **hibernate** instead. During the summer, these animals begin to store great quantities of fat in their bodies. As autumn approaches, they find a sheltered place where they can spend the winter. Now their bodies undergo a number of changes. The body temperature, which is usually about 38°C, begins to drop. Eventually it will fall to only 3° or 4°C and it will remain like this until spring. The breathing rate and heartbeat also slow down considerably. Because their bodies are working at a slow rate, little energy is needed. This means that the stored food is used up very slowly and, therefore, lasts until the spring when the animals wake up.

Some animals seem to hibernate even during the warmer parts of the year. Bats are **nocturnal** animals which sleep during the day. When they sleep, the body temperature drops and they

When the dormouse *(above)* hibernates, it curls up in a ball to keep warm. Most animals do this when they are cold. They also stretch out to keep cool on a hot day.

These ladybirds *(right)* are hibernating amongst the dead leaves on a shrub. They protect themselves from the cold by keeping close to each other, or by slipping in under the curling leaves.

The black bear *(below)* spends the winter sleeping in a den which it has excavated. During this time the bear lives off its fat. The young are born in the dens.

become **torpid**. This is not true hibernation but it does help bats to use less energy during daylight hours. In winter, when insect food is scarce, bats enter a proper state of hibernation.

The hummingbirds of South America are even more remarkable. These are the smallest of the birds with a high metabolic rate. They cannot maintain such activity for more than about twelve hours at a time and so they have to hibernate every night. Again, this is not true hibernation, but the body temperature drops and the metabolic rate slows down to conserve energy.

Some animals become inactive in hot, dry conditions. Snails are dormant during periods of drought and they seal themselves inside their shells until conditions improve. The African lungfish burrows into the mud when the water in which it lives dries up. It surrounds itself in a slimy **cocoon** to conserve moisture. Breathing takes place through a small hole in the wall of the cocoon, and the fish can survive for several months in this way. When the drought ends, the fish breaks out of its protective covering and takes up its normal life again. This type of behaviour is called **aestivation**. Some tropical frogs and toads behave in a similar way.

Life in deserts

JUST OVER TWO HUNDRED YEARS AGO, a Secretary of the Royal Society in England, Dr Blagden, carried out an interesting experiment. Together with some friends, a dog and a piece of raw steak, he entered a room where the air temperature was 126°C. Forty-five minutes later, everyone came out in good health, but the piece of steak was cooked and ready to eat.

Nearly fourteen per cent of the Earth's land area is covered by desert regions which have a high temperature and where conditions are very dry. The highest air temperature ever recorded on Earth, 58°C in the shade, was measured in the Sahara desert. Although such a high temperature has been recorded only once, temperatures often reach 50°C in the hottest parts of the world. When there is no cloud cover, heat quickly radiates back from the Earth into the sky after nightfall. When this happens, the temperature quickly drops. Such cold nights are important to the survival of desert plants and animals.

The desert regions of the world are shown in brown.

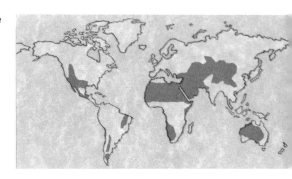

The North American jack rabbit *(bottom right)* is really a hare. The large surface area of its ears and the rich blood supply make the ears ideal as radiators for keeping the animal cool. Many desert animals have extra large ears for this reason.

Apart from a few cactus plants, the Mexican desert *(below)* appears desolate. It is hard to imagine that many animals and plants could survive. At night, animals emerge from their underground homes and hunt for food in the cool night air.

In this environment of hot temperatures and dry conditions, plants and animals have become specially adapted to survive. Many plants cope with the problem of drought by avoiding it. They survive as seeds which lie dormant in the soil, often for many years. The seeds germinate only when it rains. When this happens the plants mature quickly and produce new fruits and seeds in a short period of time. These new seeds will become the next generation of plants.

Some animals behave in a similar way

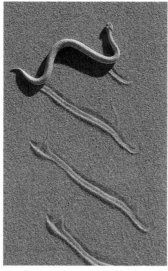

Certain species of frog burrow underground and cover themselves in a waterproof, cocoon-like sheath. They stay in this state for long periods, coming out only when it rains. After emerging from the cocoon, they mate and complete their life cycle quickly while water is still available.

Many desert plants survive drought in other ways. They often have specialized roots which collect water over as wide an area as possible. Others produce long roots which search for water at depths up to 100 m below the surface. All plants lose water through their leaves. Many cacti have spines in place of leaves to stop too much water being lost. Other plants have thick, waxy leaves for the same reason. Many larger plants, including cacti and trees, store water in their stems for use later on.

Animals in hot climates are not able to store water. However, they can conserve it. Desert rodents have specially adapted kidneys to help keep water in the body. The camel swallows the drippings from its nose to save valuable water. Some animals are even able to change their own environment and make it more humid. The kangaroo rat seals itself in its burrow during the day. The water vapour in its breath gradually accumulates, making the atmosphere of the burrow very moist. The rat also stores seeds in its burrow and the moist air softens their hard covering and makes them easier to eat.

Many desert animals can survive for long periods without water. The camel can do this but eventually it makes up for it by drinking large volumes in a very short time, often as much as 50 litres in less than twenty minutes. This is equal to the amount of petrol a driver puts into a large car when filling up at a service station. Some animals such as the addax from

(left) Most desert people are nomads. The Tuareg of North Africa are typical nomads. They live in tents which are open on one side to let the air in. The tents are often made from woven goat hair.

The sidewinder snake *(above)* is found in the deserts of Arizona, California, and Nevada. It moves across the desert by throwing loops of its body sideways.

The dromedary *(below)*, or one-humped camel, is well adapted to a desert environment. It can go for long periods without drinking. The hump absorbs heat and carries a store of fat.

the Sahara and the kangaroo rat from North America never drink water. They get all the moisture they need from the food they eat.

Apart from a shortage of water, the other main problem faced by animals in hot climates is that of overheating. Most desert animals are nocturnal and are able to take advantage of the cooler nights. They stay in the shade, underground, during the day and come out at night to find food.

Other animals have developed special ways of cooling down. Certain parts of the body are adapted as radiators for this purpose. The fennec fox from Africa and the North American jack rabbit have extra long ears. These contain many blood vessels and they provide a large surface across which heat can pass. As blood flows through the ears it brings heat from the body. This heat radiates from the ears into the surroundings. In this way, the animal cools down. The African elephant uses its large ears in the same way. When it flaps them, its body surface increases by about twenty per cent. This increased surface allows more heat to be radiated and this cools the animal.

Desert animals and plants live in the world's hottest and driest environments. Even humans have adapted to such conditions. Bedouin tribes have roamed the great Arabian Desert for thousands of years, and the hostile Kalahari has been successfully invaded by groups of Bushmen over the centuries. These special adaptations for survival in hot, dry climates are many and varied and all have evolved over very long periods of time.

Life in cold climates

VERY FEW PLANTS or animals are adapted to live in the cold, icy wastes of the Arctic or Antarctic. Even humans have been unable to live for long periods in the Antarctic. In the Arctic, the Eskimos live mainly on fish and other animals taken from the sea. Unlike the Antarctic regions, the Arctic is largely a frozen skin of ice over a rich ocean.

The animals that do live in cold climates need to be able to keep out the intense cold and keep in their own body heat. All the large animals that are found in these cold climates, such as seals, whales and polar bears, are warm-blooded mammals. This means that they produce heat within their bodies in order to keep their blood

Eskimo people have learned to copy the animals and they rub fat over their skin and use animal furs to keep out the cold.

The animals that survive in the snow and ice of the Arctic depend upon the sea for food. The same is true of the Antarctic, where the little life that exists is found around the coasts. Inland, on the glaciers and ice fields, nothing can survive to provide food for other animals. The polar seas are colder than ordinary ice because the salt in seawater prevents it from freezing at the normal temperature of 0°C. These cold oceans are rich in **nutrients**, and the microscopic plants and animals that make up **plankton**. These provide the beginning of a series of food chains.

Eskimos have adapted well to the harsh climate of the Arctic. They are good hunters, relying on fish and seals for food, clothing and oil.

(right) The husky has a thick coat which helps it to survive in very cold conditions. Huskies are hardy animals and make ideal working dogs.

at a steady temperature. To keep this heat in and stop the bitter cold from chilling them, they have a thick, outer covering to **insulate** them. The polar bear and Arctic fox both have very thick fur to keep them warm. The water-dwelling seals and whales have a very thick layer of fat, or blubber, beneath the skin. This provides them with a good insulation layer. The

Even the food chains which include large whales start off with plankton.

The lack of large predators in the Antarctic snowfields has enabled many different kinds of penguin to thrive without fear of other land animals. These strange birds cannot fly. Their short wings are used as flippers for underwater swimming. Penguins are protected from the icy

The polar bear *(left)* depends upon fish and seals for its food. It can survive in this unfriendly environment, protected from the cold by thick, greasy fur.

When the snow melts in the spring, the flat, treeless land, called tundra, comes alive with small plants. These include mosses, lichens and some small, flowering plants, such as the yellow Arctic poppy.

A 'rookery' of Adelie penguins in the Antarctic. Penguins cannot fly, but they are expert divers and swimmers. Their 'wings' have become adapted as flippers, and their feet are webbed to help them swim.

cold water by a covering of feathers and by a layer of fat similar to that of the seals.

The only plants to be found in Antarctica are tiny mosses which manage to survive on the rocks and pebbles that peep through the ice in summer. In the Arctic there are many plants which spend most of the year buried beneath the snow of Greenland, Iceland, Alaska and Siberia. In the brief but sunny days of summer, when the ice melts, they must flower and set their seed.

During most of the year the soil in which these Arctic plants live is frozen solid. When the cells of plants or animals become frozen, the water inside freezes. The sharp ice crystals burst the cell walls and kill the plant or animal. To avoid this happening the Arctic plants either go through the long, dark winter as a resistant seed with little water inside, or avoid being frozen. Many plants and animals of cold climates contain a chemical called an anti-freeze. This is very similar to the liquid used in car radiators during the winter months. The blood of many fish and other sea organisms contains such an antifreeze. This prevents their blood from turning to ice until a temperature of $-2\,°C$ is reached.

In the Arctic, many animals can avoid the grip of winter by migrating south as winter approaches. They return with the warmer days of spring to feed on the new growth of Arctic plants. After the thaw, the type of scenery that is found is called **tundra**. This is a flat, treeless type of land, covered by a host of mosses, lichens and dwarf bushes. Tundra can be a familiar part of high mountains anywhere in the world, not just at the poles. The Alps in Europe are well known for their brightly coloured alpine flowers which appear after the snow melts. Most adaptations mentioned for the polar regions also apply to high mountain tops. The same problem of cold and food supply can affect life even on mountains like Mount Kilimanjaro, in Africa, which is almost on the Equator. Even in difficult or harsh conditions, nature produces plants and animals that can survive.

Life on islands

THE MAIN FEATURE of many islands is that they are difficult places for plants and animals to reach. Because of this they have special appeal to those scientists who study living organisms. The Galapagos Islands in the Pacific Ocean form an interesting group. When Charles Darwin landed there in 1835 he discovered a very unusual collection of plants and animals. This visit aroused scientists' interest, and these islands have since provided a great deal of information about island life.

The nearest land to the Galapagos Islands is 960 km away. The only organisms that are able to cross such huge distances of ocean are those that can fly, swim or float on bits of driftwood. Very occasionally, a freak storm may blow or wash ashore some other type of animal or plant seed or seedling. Some plants are adapted to reaching remote islands. The coconut palm has

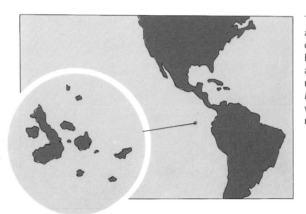

The Galapagos Islands, which are all volcanic, lie in the Pacific ocean, scattered across the Equator. They became famous after the visit, in 1835, of the naturalist Charles Darwin, in *HMS Beagle*. His theory of evolution was confirmed by discoveries he made in this lonely island group.

One of the strange species that Darwin found on the Galapagos Islands was the iguana. This huge lizard grows up to 2 m in length. There are two types on the islands, the marine iguana and the land iguana (shown below).

large 'floats' around the seed, or coconut as we call it. These floats carry the seeds across the ocean, and some may become washed up on remote shores, far from where their journey started.

We call small areas of land 'islands' because they are cut off, or isolated, from the main parts of the world. Islands can be formed by volcanoes rising from the seabed, by coral reefs building upwards, or by changes in sea level. After the last ice age, melting ice and snow swelled the oceans and swallowed up low-lying valleys to leave higher ground as islands. Animals and plants that reach islands are usually stranded there, and quickly learn to make use of the food resources, or adapt.

On the Galapagos Islands, Darwin found fourteen different species of a small bird called a finch. These looked similar in many respects except for their beaks. Each species had a certain shape of beak which helped it to catch and eat one type of food only. He found insect-eaters with sharp, pointed beaks and seed-eaters with broad, strong beaks. Scientists believe that some of the first birds to reach the Galapagos Islands were a few storm-blown finches. These first birds would have had no competition for food because there were no other birds on the new island. At the beginning, the birds probably ate a wide range of different foods. However, over many thousands of years, some of the finches gradually adapted and began to specialize in eating one type of food. Within each group, the individual birds with beaks best shaped to deal with a specific food would be at an advantage. Gradually, the beak shape of a particular group of finches changed from the beak shape of the original few birds.

Darwin called this natural selection, where only the best adapted birds survive. Each group of finches was filling a gap, or **niche**, which would normally be filled by other species and types of bird.

The example of the Galapagos Islands shows us how animals and plants adapt to their new surroundings. In a similar way, the island of Madagascar was isolated from Africa before many types of animal had developed, or evolved there. Tree-living lemurs are mostly found in Madagascar, where they take the place of the true monkeys which exist on the African mainland.

Islands need not be small pieces of land. Australia is really an island in the biological sense, but it is so large that we call it a continent. In isolation, there have developed in Australia many animal and plant forms which are unlike anything in the rest of the world. The best known are the **marsupials**. These are animals that carry their young in pouches until they are old enough to feed themselves. There are marsupial mice, rats, wolves, cats and there is even a marsupial mole. The gap, or niche, occupied by grazing animals in the rest of the

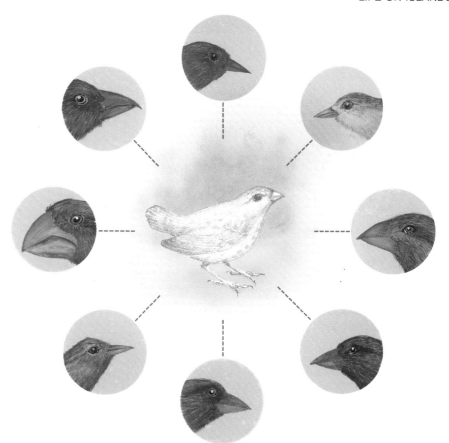

The finches on the Galapagos Islands provided Darwin with an important clue to his theory of natural selection. He found many different species, each with a distinctive beak shape adapted to a particular type of food.

The isolation of islands, such as Bora-Bora in the Pacific *(left)*, has led to the evolution of a wide variety of plants and animals. In a habitat where there is no competition for food, the plants and animals are each able to fill a gap, or niche, normally filled by other species.

world, is filled in Australia by kangaroos and wallabies.

One of the problems faced by organisms living on islands is the possibility of dying out, or extinction. On some islands in the Pacific there were no large flesh-eating animals. Some of the birds which reached these habitats gradually lost the power of flight and became wingless. The dodo once lived on Mauritius, and is a well-known example of a wingless bird that could not compete with the pigs, goats and rats later

The dodo, now extinct.

brought in by human settlers. The settlers themselves caught and ate these helpless birds. The balance of life on an island is very delicate and, if this is disturbed by humans or by new animals, then species die out, never to be replaced. Another rule of island life is that the larger the island, the more species you will find there.

So far we have thought of islands as patches of land surrounded by water. However, all the features of islands also apply to a wood surrounded by vast areas of wheat fields, or to mountains rising up out of hot, dry plains. Mount Kenya and Mount Kilimanjaro are really 'islands' in the middle of the East African savannah. Each has its own particular plants and animals, different from those on the plains below. These are biological islands and are really isolated patches of natural countryside surrounded by a different environment. Naturalists are worried that we may lose more species of plants and animals from these land-locked islands, because of their isolation.

Seashore life

THE STUDY OF ANIMALS and plants and where they live is called **ecology**. It is a science which tries to understand how living organisms fit in with each other and their surroundings. People who work on these problems are called ecologists and the place they choose to study – it may be a wood or a field or a freshwater pond – is called an **ecosystem**.

A great many animals and plants live in the sea and although a lot of people have studied them, there is still a great deal more to learn. One reason for this is that the sea is a difficult place to work in, even for experts. It is deep, often cold and dangerous and we humans need to take with us air for breathing.

However, there is one part which is easy to visit and that is the seashore. Here we can stand

1 lugworms
2 cockles
3 sea belt
4 mermaid's purse
5 shore crab
6 knotted wrack
7 razor-clam
8 bladder wrack
9 spiral wrack
10 limpets
11 sea anemones
12 acorn barnacles
13 channelled wrack
14 prawn
15 butterfish
16 mussels
17 brittle star
18 edible crab
19 starfish
20 sand goby
21 sea aster

safely on dry land and look at the inhabitants of a very different world.

It does not take long to realize that our beaches are full of animals and plants living in a special kind of order, with each well-suited to the life it leads. Their world is not an easy one. The sea is a powerful force as it crashes over rocks, pounds against cliffs and glides over flat beaches of sand and pebbles, rolling them to and fro. Added to this is the large amount of salt in the water itself.

The best time to explore is when the tide is out and everything is calm for a while. The most obvious things to discover are seaweeds. These lie flat and unsupported by the water but have tough skins which protect them from being eaten or from drying out in the wind and sun. Anchored to rocks or pieces of driftwood, the position seaweeds occupy on the beach depends on how long they can last out of water. Some

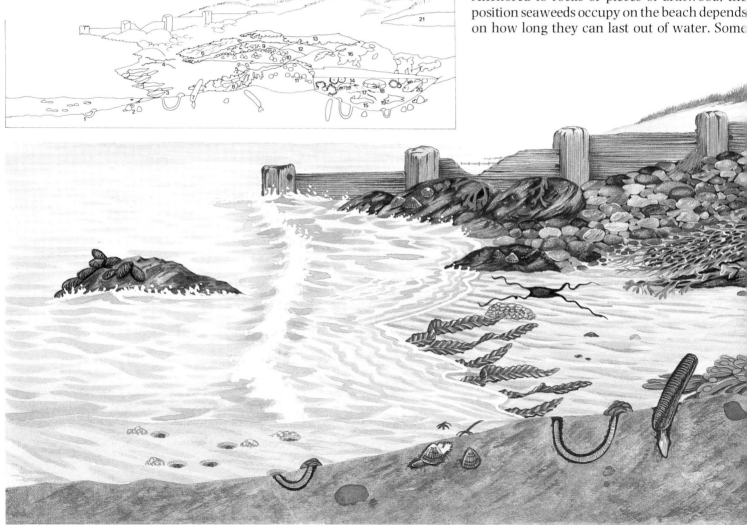

are better at this than are others. The 'wrack' seaweeds are a good example.

The channelled wrack lives furthest up the beach near the high-tide mark. Because of its position, it is exposed for the longest period of time at low tide. Lower down the beach, spiral and knotted wrack can be found. The bladder wrack lives still closer to the sea. In the water for most of its life and exposed only by the lowest of tides is the sea belt, with its single stems up to 2 m long.

Rock pools are the treasure-chests of the seashore. Some of them may have fish, crabs and shrimps left behind by the falling tide. Many of the rocks are covered in shellfish such as limpets and barnacles, which are **crustaceans**. These seal themselves up and stick on tightly when exposed to the air. The more rubbery, dark red lumps are sea anemones, so-called because when they are underwater they fan out lots of arms which look like the flowerhead of the plant they are named after.

On the flat and exposed beaches there are hardly any plants and most of the animals are safely buried beneath the surface. Lugworms take packets of sand down with them and sift through them looking for food. Sand-masons are also worms, but they build a protective case out of shell fragments and sand, stuck together with a sticky glue. They can be more adventurous than lugworms. Razor-clams are long and thin and have such a strong foothold that it is very difficult to pull them out of the sand. Perhaps the most plentiful shellfish is the cockle and scientists have estimated that some of the larger beaches may contain populations of more than 450 million hiding in the mud. Here they wait for the sea to cover them up so they can start feeding again. In addition, many wading birds visit the seashore to search for food.

The effect of the sea does not stop at the highest tide mark. Beyond that are sand dunes and salt marshes with their special kinds of plants and animals. These are also dependent on the sea for their way of life. One of the changes that ecologists look for has been made because these organisms are now better at living out of the sea rather than in it. The sea is an important place for the future. It covers nearly three quarters of the Earth's surface. If we could learn to farm it properly for plant and animal food, a lot of our own problems on dry land might be solved.

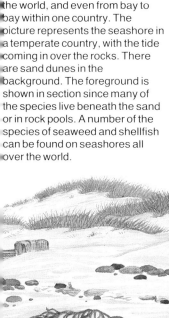

Seashore life varies throughout the world, and even from bay to bay within one country. The picture represents the seashore in a temperate country, with the tide coming in over the rocks. There are sand dunes in the background. The foreground is shown in section since many of the species live beneath the sand or in rock pools. A number of the species of seaweed and shellfish can be found on seashores all over the world.

Life in oceans

OCEANS differ from seas mainly in size, depth and openness. There are five main oceans of the world: the Atlantic, the Pacific, the Indian, the Arctic and the great southern ocean around Antarctica. Over two-thirds of the Earth's surface is covered by ocean, with an average depth of 3.6 km. The oceans and seas contain a much greater variety of animal and plant groups than is found on land.

Sunlight is important to all forms of life, because it is used by plants to make food. This food is then used by animals that eat the plants. In sea water, sunlight can penetrate only to a depth of about 200 m. This restricts the depth at which plants can grow.

In coastal waters and shallow seas there are giant forms of seaweed growing from the seabed, and every rock is coated with plant life. In the oceans, the seabed is in darkness and plants are absent. Instead, many of the plants in oceans are tiny, single-celled ones which float in the upper layers. These are called **phytoplankton**. Just like the land plants, they contain chlorophyll. Providing the sea water contains plenty of nutrients, the phytoplankton can trap sunlight and convert its energy into food.

One of the main problems faced by ocean life is keeping afloat. The microscopic size of the phytoplankton helps them to do this, aided by the upward-moving ocean currents.

Not all ocean plants are tiny. Part of the Atlantic Ocean, known as the Sargasso Sea, is a thick mass of floating sargassum seaweed. This does not drift all over the Atlantic but is kept in one place by ocean currents. The Sargasso Sea is home for a whole series of different creatures including the young stages of the freshwater eel. The female eels travel across the Atlantic from Europe to mate and lay their eggs in the sargassum weed, and the young eels have to make the journey back once they are large enough.

Feeding on the phytoplankton are the equally tiny, single-celled animals called **zooplankton**. Many of these have beautiful 'skeletons' or 'shells' which help them to float. Some of the best known groups of zooplankton are the **radiolarians** and **foraminiferans**. Their skeletons are filled with small holes and hollow spines containing a liquid which is lighter than

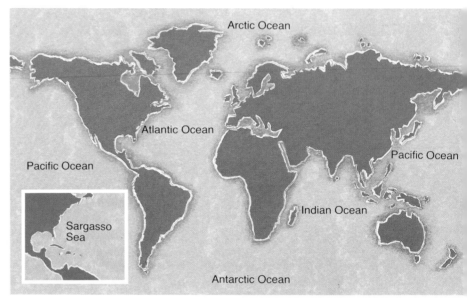

The five main oceans of the world cover over two-thirds of the Earth's surface, and contain a great variety of animal and plant life. The Sargasso Sea (inset), in the Atlantic Ocean, takes its name from the thick masses of sargassum seaweed that cover the surface. It is in this weed that eels from Europe lay their eggs.

Zooplankton are tiny, single-celled animals that are able to float in the top layers of the ocean because they are filled with a liquid that is lighter than seawater.

sea water. This is how they keep afloat. The empty 'shells' of foraminifera have, over millions of years, built up into the rock we know as chalk. Other types of zooplankton animals keep afloat by using whip-like propellers, or flagella.

The food chains which exist in the oceans are similar to those on land. The plants, or producers, are the phytoplankton. The main herbivores, or grazers, are the zooplankton. The first real, predatory animals are the masses of microscopic larvae, which are the young stages, of many other sea animals. Almost all sea animals feed, at one time in their lives, as small larvae in

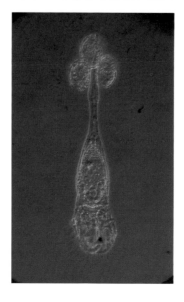

The phytoplankton that live in the upper, sunlit layer of the ocean form the basis of the food chains. These are grazed by zooplankton which, in turn, provide food for the larvae of other sea animals. These larvae become prey for small fish in the upper ocean layers. In the deeper, darker waters deep-sea fish live on smaller fish and other sea creatures. The animals that live in the seabed catch the debris that falls from above. The cycle is completed by deep currents that well up to the surface waters, carrying nutrients essential for the growth of phytoplankton.

the plankton layer. Even the eggs of fishes hatch into tiny fry that live for a short time in the upper plankton layers. Most of these young animals will end up as a meal for another fish or squid. In turn, small fish are eaten by larger fish and so on. This part of ocean life takes place in the surface layers reached by sunlight.

The deepest parts of the oceans are dark, cold places. Here all life has to rely upon food that sinks from the upper layers. We can think of the ocean food web as being in two parts. The upper, sunlit, surface waters and the deep, dark waters where no plants can grow. The extraordinary deep-sea fish with their huge jaws and coloured lights exist by eating other smaller fish and other sea creatures. The seabed is dotted with strange animals called sea-lilies, with

spreading tentacles to catch the falling dead bodies of plankton. Other animals feed on the decaying droppings, or **detritus**, that rains down upon them from above.

As in all natural food webs, there has to be a return of nutrients to the beginning of the cycle. In the ocean this is done by cold, deep currents which push up to the surface waters. These currents carry a mass of nutrients essential for the growth of phytoplankton. Wherever these currents rise to the surface, that part of the ocean is very rich in nutrients and phytoplankton. The presence of large amounts of phytoplankton attracts fish in large numbers. Such areas are visited by fishing boats, or trawlers, from all over the world to gather the rich harvest of the ocean.

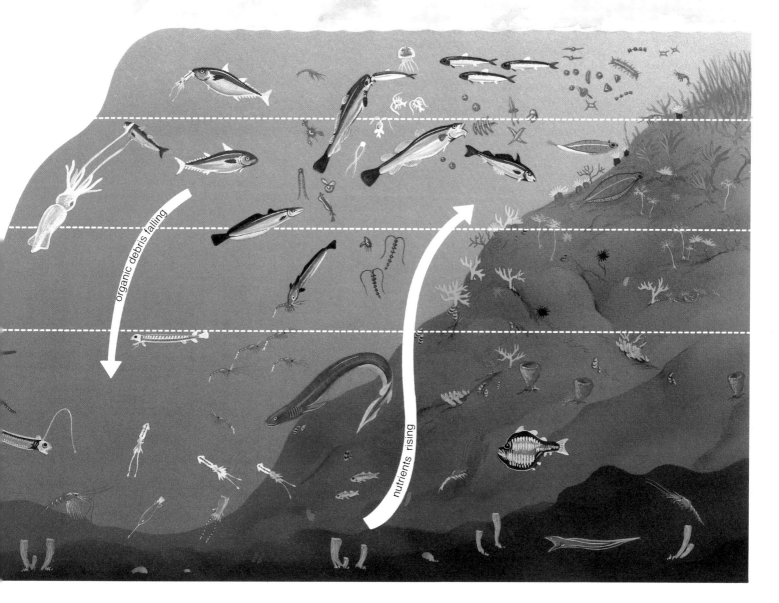

organic debris falling

nutrients rising

Freshwater life

RUSHING STREAMS, rivers, ponds and lakes make up the fresh water environment. Each of these presents a different set of problems for the animals and plants which live in them.

Life in fresh water depends on three factors: how fast the water is flowing, how much oxygen there is in the water and how rich the water is in food materials.

Water must have oxygen dissolved in it, in order to support life. Although living totally submerged, animals still need oxygen to survive. This dissolved oxygen must be taken from the water, and fish do this by passing the water over their gills. Here oxygen is taken from the water, and poisonous waste material, carbon dioxide, is taken from the body and passed to the water.

Plants also need oxygen. Some live with leaves floating on the water or growing up out of it, and such plants take their oxygen from the air. Other plants live totally submerged and absorb oxygen from the water over their whole surface. Many also take their food materials from the water in this way. Roots serve mainly to anchor the plant, and often have little to do with taking in food materials.

Plants also take carbon dioxide from the water. Like land-living plants, they use this, together with water and other minerals, in the presence of sunlight, to make their food. This process is called photosynthesis.

The range of life in a river changes substantially throughout its course. This imaginary river in Africa shows life in three typical sections. Near its source (1), in hilly country, the river is narrow and fast flowing. Downstream (2) the river tends to widen and the current is more gentle. In the lagoon or shallow lake (3) there is hardly any water movement and plant life becomes more varied.

Fast-flowing streams and rivers are usually found in hilly country and on mountain sides. Such water splashes over rocks and boulders and is rich in oxygen. It is also likely to be cold and rich in food materials. Life is not easy in such conditions. Fish have to fight against the current to stop being swept away – only fish such as trout, which are strong swimmers, are able to survive. Plants, too, have to be firmly anchored or they are washed away. Birds may live in and around such streams; one, the dipper, actually walks under the water on the bottom of the stream or swims about, using its wings, as it searches for food. Other animals that survive are those without backbones. These are called invertebrates. Many of these invertebrates are the immature stages of insects, such as dragonflies, which are readily recognized as adults. They seek shelter in and among the boulders and when mature they crawl out of the water on to a stone or leaf and change into the adult form. The variety of life in these upland streams is not great.

As the contours of the land become less steep, so the speed of water in rivers slows down. Being swept away becomes less of a problem. More types of fish, such as roach and chub, both slower swimmers, cope better under these conditions. In these areas some birds, including

kingfishers and herons, feed in the water without swimming. Fish-hunting otters and, in tropical parts of the world, crocodiles and turtles, find their homes in slower rivers. Plant life becomes more varied and, as the rivers approach the sea, they become easier places in which to live.

Ponds and lakes have little or no water movement. They receive their food supplies and their oxygen from inflowing streams and rivers. The amount of oxygen and food materials in the water is at its highest during winter and spring when rainfall is heavy. Fish do not have to waste energy battling against the current, and plants do not need to be rooted to the bottom. Many plants are free-floating and may be found near the surface of the deepest waters. Some birds dive in a search for food, while grebes dive and swim to catch small fish – as do pelicans, in warmer parts of the world. Some ducks will dive in deeper water while others dabble in the mud at the water's edge in their search for food.

In hot countries, ponds and lakes may dry up. This causes problems for animals and plants living there. Many of them die, but others are able to survive by forming cysts around themselves or by burying themselves in the mud. In these still or slow waters live forms of life, both animals and plants, that are too small to be seen by the naked eye. They are called plankton and are very important because they are a food source for other animals. Flocks of pink flamingoes search the shallow, warm waters in certain parts of the tropics feeding on this plankton. Small fish and other invertebrates eat plankton and they, in turn, are eaten by larger,

predatory fish such as pike and perch. The smaller fish and some of the larger ones are in turn eaten by larger animals, such as otters, herons and ospreys. This dependence of one animal on another is known as a food chain. It is important that such chains are not broken if much of the life in fresh water is to survive. Not all the animals that live in the fresh water are flesh-eaters. The hippopotamus, found in African lakes and rivers, and the water vole are both vegetarians. Many of the invertebrates are scavengers, living off dead animal and plant material.

Some animals live for part of their lives in fresh water and for the other part on land. These are the amphibians, animals such as frogs, toads and salamanders. Their breathing systems are adapted to this way of life and they have both gills and lungs at different stages of growth. Apart from using lungs, frogs are able to absorb oxygen over their body surface, but only when the surface is moist. If their skin becomes dry, they suffocate, and so they must live in damp places, close to water. Water is also essential for their reproduction.

Life in fresh water depends on many things, above all the need for clean water with sufficient oxygen. Without this, life becomes impossible and the fresh water soon becomes stagnant, smelly and lifeless.

1	lungfish
2	white headed duck
3	dragon fly
4	pied kingfisher
5	diving beetle
6	caddis fly
7	leaf fish
8	egret
9	upside down catfish
10	osprey
11	Mozambique cichlid
12	zebra cichlid
13	soft-shelled turtles
14	crocodile
15	electric catfish
16	elephant fish
17	darter
18	pintailed sand grouse
19	hippo
20	banded jewel fish
21	white-spotted cichlid
22	knife fish
23	clawed toad
24	galaxias
25	African otter
26	may fly
27	pied wagtail
28	black bass
29	shrimp
30	caddis fly
31	dragonfly larva
32	grey wagtail
33	poison frog
34	Asiatic salamander

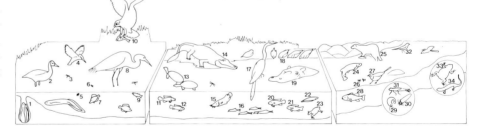

Life in forests

Much of the earth's land surface is still covered by forests of various kinds. These forest areas were once even more widespread, but gradually the trees have been cut down to provide more land for farming. The human population has been growing rapidly and farmers have had to produce more food.

Forests contain large numbers of organisms. Groups of animals and other plants live together in harmony with the trees, making up

what is called the forest ecosystem. This system supports itself and, if humans did not interfere, would go on for ever. As the old animals and plants die, young ones grow up to take their places.

Trees will grow in most places, apart from the frozen wastes of the polar regions, the tops of high mountains and in deserts. If it is left alone for a long time, any patch of bare ground will become covered by trees. First of all, the ground becomes covered in non-woody plants, some of which live for only a year. These are called **annuals**. As time passes, shrubs become established, and many of the original colonizers

The main forest belts of the world.

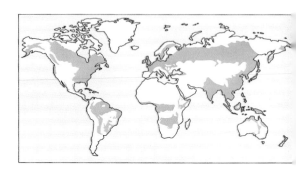

Compared with other types of forests, conditions in tropical rain forests hardly ever change. This is because they are close to the equator. The climate is hot and, because of the heavy rainfall and dense vegetation, it is humid. The variety of life in the jungle is enormous, with many thousands of different species found in a small area.

cannot survive in the shade created. In time, trees will invade the area and they, in turn, overshadow many of the shrubs. These trees grow in size, and so a forest gradually develops. Trees are generally slow in growing, and may live for many years. For example, there is a species of conifer tree growing in California that is known to have a lifespan of at least 5000 years. Gradually, as old trees die, new ones grow up to take their place. In this way, forest areas are able to remain very stable environments.

The conditions in which trees grow vary from region to region. This is because the climate varies in different parts of the world. As we pass northwards and southwards from the Equator, the climate becomes gradually colder. As a result, we find belts of vegetation made up of plants that survive best under these different climatic conditions. Close to the Equator, there are massive tropical rain forests made up of huge trees. These grow so close together that their leaves prevent much of the Sun's light from reaching the forest floor. Smaller trees and shrubs grow under the **canopy** of the tall trees. These smaller trees reach about half the height of their giant neighbours. Beneath them, on the forest floor, there is a third layer of low-growing shrubs and other non-woody plants.

There are no seasons in these Equatorial regions. The temperature is hot and there is a high rainfall. Conditions for growth are equally good throughout the year. Many of the trees are **evergreen** and keep their leaves all the year round. Others lose theirs at certain times of the year, but this is not in response to seasonal changes. These rain forests contain large numbers of different kinds of animals. Insects abound and many of them grow to a large size and are brightly coloured. Some of the birdwing

butterflies in the rain forests of New Guinea have a wing span of 30 cm. Many brightly coloured birds and mammals live in the forest canopy, where they feed on the rich supply of flowers and fruits. On the forest floor are found other animals, including large predators such as jaguars and leopards.

In the **temperate** forest zone, trees respond to the seasons. During the winter they lose their leaves. This is an adaptation to help the trees survive the worst of the winter's frost, ice and snow. When warmer temperatures return in spring, then the trees burst into leaf again. Deer, bison and wild boar graze within these forests. Hawks, owls, polecats and foxes are among the flesh-eaters. There are many birds, some of which eat insects, while others feed on fruit and seeds.

In the northern **coniferous** forest zone the trees have to be able to withstand extreme ranges of climate. Summers may be hot and dry, whereas winters are very cold. Conifers do not shed their leaves in winter and, because of this, they still lose some water through their surfaces. However, conifer leaves are specially modified so that water loss is reduced as much as possible. This is important because, when the ground is frozen, water is not readily available to the trees. Animals living in these forests include bears, lynx, squirrels and foxes. Predatory birds, such as eagles and owls, are also found there. Beavers make their lodges in the rivers of the forest.

Forests support themselves. The death of plants and animals, and their decaying remains, is an important part of this process. Many small animals and various types of fungi live among the thick layer of dead leaves, twigs and even large branches and trunks, on the forest floor. They break down this plant material to provide

Life in temperate forests responds to the changing seasons. Scenes of plentiful growth during spring and summer are replaced with the fallen leaves and bare branches of deciduous trees during the winter months. Animal life is abundant although few of the larger species such as bison and wild boar are now found.

The northern coniferous forests have to contend with severe winters. Snow covers the ground for about half the year, and the extreme cold threatens all life. Many of the animals hibernate or migrate south - all need to conserve their valuable energy, since food is scarce in the long winter months.

energy for themselves. At the same time, they release valuable nutrients into the soil for other plants to use. In turn, when these animals and plants die, others feed on their remains, and the cycle continues. Animals in forests may be flesh-eating carnivores, or may live off the vegetation growing in the forest. In both cases they leave their droppings on the forest floor. This also contributes towards the recycling of food materials. Population levels of both animals and plants are controlled by this cycle, each depending on the others for life. In a well-established forest this natural system would go on for ever. Only a change of climate or human interference can endanger it.

Pollution of the environment

In the natural world every living organism has its place in the order of things. The materials and chemicals that make up living organisms return, in due course, to the soil or the air when the organisms die. There is a special group of plants and animals which break down, or **decompose**, dead bodies. We call this natural waste **biodegradable**, and this means that it can be broken down by living organisms. The natural decomposers range from microscopic bacteria and fungi to insects and large **scavengers**, such as the hyena. All of these carry out the task of removing the remains of dead plants and animals. Without them we would be surrounded by the rotting remains of dead matter.

As human civilization developed, the natural balance was upset. The first humans began to change the environment with tools and the use of fire. Forests were chopped down, and the land cleared for agriculture. Settlements were created, and this led to the build-up of piles of material which had been discarded as rubbish. Some of this rubbish, broken pots and tools, could not be decomposed, and so formed the very first type of **pollution**. In the broadest sense, anything which cannot be broken down by natural means can be called pollution.

When the world population was small, the effect of a few rubbish tips was not very serious. As large towns and cities came into being, the growing amount of rubbish and **sewage** be-

Griffon vultures feeding on the remains of a dead animal. These birds are scavengers, acting as natural decomposers. They remove the remains that might otherwise cause pollution and disease.

Chemical waste from a phosphate factory pours into the sea. The waste alters the balance of salts in sea water, and therefore damages or kills living organisms.

came a health hazard. Rotting and uneaten food attracted rats and this led to disease. In the Middle Ages such pollution was very dangerous. Millions of people died from bubonic plague, typhoid and cholera, as plagues of these diseases spread through many countries.

As mankind became more industrial, the problems of pollution increased. The role of industry is to convert raw materials and chemicals into the goods which society demands, for example, plastics, paper and metal goods. In this process, factories produce waste, much of which is not biodegradable. Many of these by-products are fairly harmless in small quantities, but are very dangerous when present in large amounts. Over the years, materials like these have been washed away into rivers where they upset the balance of life. Manufacturers did not worry about this until it began to harm the environment.

One of the first signs that we were poisoning our own world came with an **insecticide** called DDT. It was used to kill mosquitoes, and thus helped in reducing malarial disease. However, once in the soil, DDT could not be broken down by decomposers. In time the chemical passed up the various food chains from insects to fish, fish to birds, and eventually even began to poison humans.

Today, pollution is all around us. One of the most worrying forms of pollution at the present time is the so-called **acid rain**. This is caused by sulphur compounds in smoke dissolving in rainwater to form weak acids. As the polluted rain fills rivers and lakes, the acidity upsets the natural balance. In parts of eastern North America, for example, there are lakes which have lost many of the plants and animals which once lived there. The acid rain also kills off plants on land and causes trees to lose their leaves.

Modern fertilizers seemed a good idea at first, since they helped the farmers to produce more food. As the fertilizers washed into rivers and ponds, they produced rich growths of algae and other plants. When these multiplied, they began to use up all the oxygen in the water and very soon the fish died.

This is typical of many pollution problems. We only become aware of the pollution when the damage has been done. We appear to be walking a tightrope, and if we continue to disturb the balance of nature we will increasingly become victims of our own products.

Three common forms of pollution. Waste chemicals from factories *(below)* pollute fresh water. Crop-spraying *(top)* with insecticides may help the farmer, but sometimes causes long-term damage to the environment. *(right)* The effect of acid rain on trees.

Conservation of species

LIFE HAS EXISTED on Earth for more than 3000 million years. In that time many millions of different kinds of animals and plants – on the land, in the sea and in the air – have come and gone. The human species is just one of those still alive today. In the last few thousand years humans have moved into all parts of the globe. To get what he wants for himself Man has destroyed much of the world around him.

One of the most famous examples of human destruction is the dodo. It once lived on the small Indian Ocean island of Mauritius. This island was first discovered in 1598, but in just one hundred years the dodo was made extinct by human activity. The invaders caused damage and killed the birds, but so too did the cats, dogs and rats they brought with them. The flightless dodos had no escape and by 1700 there were none left.

An Indian rhinoceros. The Rhino family consists of five species, all of which now risk extinction. They first appeared some 50 million years ago. One prehistoric type stood 5 m tall and was 7 m long. They seldom stray far from water, feeding mainly on grass, shrubs and aquatic plants.

The passenger-pigeon (left) was a migratory bird that became extinct in 1914. Blame for this has been put on human beings who slaughtered them by the thousand.

Nearly all of the birds that are now extinct lived on islands. But one example shows how even birds living in enormous numbers on big continents can be lost because of mankind. This is the story of the passenger-pigeon. At the beginning of the 1800s there were millions of these lovely birds living among the oak and beech forests of North America. Reports of more than 1000 million birds together were not un-

common! They would form flocks in the sky which were up to 8 km wide and 200 km long. Sometimes they passed in front of the Sun in such numbers that midday became almost as dark as midnight. But human beings caught and killed millions of the birds and by 1880 many of the usual breeding places were empty. It was too late to save the passenger-pigeon. The pigeons needed to live in huge flocks, and when these were broken up and the numbers reduced, the birds could not survive much longer. The last passenger-pigeon, named Martha, died in an American zoo in 1914. It belonged to a species that only a few years before had been considered one of the most common birds in the world.

The dodo and the passenger-pigeon may have been lost for ever, but we have learned many important lessons from their sad stories.

This century has seen a great many people working very hard to save animals and plants from the same fate as that of the dodo. Several international organizations have been set up for

his purpose. The World Wildlife Fund is perhaps the best known of these, and it is particularly famous for its work to save the giant panda in China and the tiger in India. Another organization, the International Union for the Conservation of Nature (IUCN), prepares lists of animals that desperately need protection and publishes these in the *Red Data Book*. Most countries also have their own national conservation societies.

Such organizations play a very important role in conservation. They advise governments on ways to protect their countries' wildlife. They help to set up reserves and national parks, and they try to stop the thoughtless destruction of the places where rare animals and plants live

Humans have hunted many species to the point of extinction. The tiger *(above)*, was once common throughout Asia, but is now endangered. Fewer than one hundred of these Spanish imperial eagles *(right)* now survive.

The stripping of vegetation deprives animals of their natural environment. These hills in Madagascar *(above)* were once covered in forest. Clearance of this type can lead to severe erosion, resulting in virtual desert.

The temptation for human beings to dig up the fine lady slipper orchid for their gardens has resulted in it becoming the rarest plant in Britain. Only two known sites remain where it grows in the wild. It is now a protected species.

wild. They also raise money so that scientists can carry out studies, because the more we know about rare plants and animals, the more likely we are to be able to help them.

Zoos, too, play a part in conservation. They enable scientists to observe animals very closely and they provide places where animals can breed in safety. They also help to make us all aware of many animals that we will probably never have the chance to see in the wild. But it would be a pity if these animals lived only in zoos and nowhere else in the world because of our selfishness.

We all have a vital part to play in the future of the world's wildlife. The world belongs to all living creatures, including mankind. If we destroy the world for others, we eventually destroy it for ourselves.

Summary

WE HAVE SEEN something of how life came about and how animals and plants survive and react as members of the living world. Life began in the seas but now extends to the highest mountains. Since the first single-celled plants came into being, some 1000 million years ago, our planet has been transformed. Plants have changed our atmosphere from one of suffocating gases to one which contains life-giving oxygen. The rocks which make up the Earth's surface have been broken down and held together as soil by the roots of plants. The cycles of growth and decay help to recycle materials such as nitrogen, carbon and other essential nutrients.

Each plant and animal has to fight, or compete, with all other individuals for a place in life. Those that are best suited to their environment survive and increase in numbers, while those that fail become extinct. These laws of nature have created the vast richness of living forms we see around us today. Ever since the first cells developed in the seas, organisms have been changing as their world went through periods of drought, ice-ages and flooding. The time scale of life is difficult to imagine. When we say that insects have been on Earth for 380 million years, the information means little until we learn that humans have existed only for the last 60 000 years.

Humans have always thought themselves apart from other forms of life. However, we have seen how our own species is descended from ape-like ancestors and is, therefore, just another type of animal. In our short time on Earth we have had an immense effect upon the rest of life. Once we had built huts and discovered fire, we began to use, or **exploit**, the living world. We felled the primeval forests which once covered much of northern Europe and replaced natural plants with crops. We hunted dangerous animals, or those that threatened our own domestic animals, until they became extinct. All in all, our history is one of changing the world around us.

At first, the forests were endless and the few

The human race has taken it upon itself to manage the world. We landscape it, change it, and sometimes severely damage it. The punishment that our Earth receives may seem to have little effect on our day-to-day lives at present. Should we continue destroying our valuable forests for short-term gains, scientists believe that the long-term result will bring about a great imbalance of nature. Quite simply this will cause changes in the Earth's atmosphere and weather, and the extinction of many of the Earth's animals.

More than half of the world's ten million plants and animal species live in the jungle. The alarms have been raised, but even so an estimated 150 000 square kilometres of tropical rain forest is being removed each year. If this rate is continued, the environment of planet Earth will be in danger.

sticks of firewood that were removed made little difference. The ever-increasing numbers of people on Earth meant that more food and more fuel were needed. To provide these, we have had to destroy much of the natural tree cover of our world. At this very moment an area of tropical rain-forest is being cut down to create space on which to grow food or to build roads. In doing this, we are killing thousands of animals and plants, some species of which may become extinct. Much more serious is the change in weather that the removal of rain-forests is causing.

Left to its own devices, nature can heal the wounds, but only if given time. If humans are to survive, we must come to terms with Nature and learn to respect our rich inheritance. We are the products of natural evolution, but now we have the power to control our future. Let us hope that we do it wisely.

Glossary

abdomen: the lower part of the body, or belly.

acid rain: rainwater *polluted* by waste fumes in the air, usually sulphur dioxide, which upsets the chemical balance of fresh water and can kill plants and animals.

adapt: to change to suit new conditions.

aestivation: the act of going into a long period of *torpor* during hot, dry periods, usually when water is very scarce.

albumen: the clear liquid surrounding and protecting the yolk.

algae: small simple *plants* that usually live in water.

amino acid: an *organic* acid needed by all living things for growth and the replacement of dead cells. *Proteins* are made of different amino acids.

ammonia: a gas, a compound of *nitrogen* and hydrogen.

amoeba: a simple animal with a single *cell* and no fixed shape, living in water.

amphibian: an animal, such as a frog, that breeds and begins its life in water but, as an adult, develops lungs and can breathe air on land.

annual: a plant which grows from seed, reproduces itself and dies, all in a single year.

anther: the part of a plant which produces *pollen*.

antidote: a drug which counteracts the effect of a poison.

asexual reproduction: the reproduction of an exact copy of itself by a single *organism*.

atmosphere: the mixture of gases (the air) which surrounds the Earth and is necessary for life on the planet.

bacteria: very simple forms of life made of a single *cell* or a small group of cells.

biodegradable: able to be decomposed by the action of *bacteria* and other *organisms*.

biological clock: a natural awareness of time shown in the behaviour of some animals.

bioluminescence: the production of light by living things.

caddis-fly: a small fly whose *larvae* live in water in special cases which they make from hollow stems and stones.

calcium carbonate: the compound which forms chalk and limestone, as well as eggshells.

camouflage: protective colouring or pattern that makes animals hard to see.

canopy: a dense, shady cover formed over a forest by the leaves of trees growing close together.

carbon dioxide: a gas found in the air. It forms the bubbles in fizzy drinks.

caribou: a large, deer-like animal found in northern North America.

carnivore: an animal that eats only other animals.

cell: the unit from which the bodies of all animals and plants are built.

chemical energy: the energy stored in a substance which is released during a chemical reaction.

chemofossil: the remains of an animal or plant found in a layer of rock in the form of *organic* compounds which made up its *cells*.

chitin: the material which forms the hard outer coverings of insects and the shells of their eggs.

chlorophyll: a substance found in plants which is used to capture energy from the Sun in *photosynthesis*.

cilia: microscopic hairs used by some single-celled animals to paddle themselves through water.

circadian: twenty-four hourly.

classification: a system of arranging different things in classes, or types, according to the ways in which they are similar, in order to study and understand them.

cocoon: a case of spun threads made by an insect *larva*, inside which it changes into an adult, such as a moth; any protective covering an animal makes for itself.

conifer: a tree, such as a pine, that produces cones.

coniferous: a word that means cone-bearing and describes a forest full of pines and fir trees.

copulation: the mating of two animals during which the male's *sperm* may *fertilize* the egg of the female.

crustacean: an animal, such as a shrimp, barnacle or crab.

curare: a poison made from the bark of certain South American trees.

cuticle: the strong outer casing of insects.

cyanide: a poisonous chemical compound.

cyclic: happening in a regular, repeated order.

cyst: a tough, non-living *membrane*.

deciduous: plants which lose their leaves in winter or before dry weather.

decompose: to break down into simple substances.

deoxyribonucleic acid (DNA): a complex *organic* acid, found in all living things, in which the characteristics of the species are passed from one generation to the next.

detritus: material formed from decaying *organisms*.

digit: a finger or toe.

disruptive camouflage: camouflage in the form of stripes or spots, which hides the animal by making its outline less clear against the background.

ecology: the study of the relationship between animals and plants and the places they live in.

ecosystem: any part of the natural world that exists without support from outside.

ectoparasite: a *parasite* that lives on the outside of its host's body.

electron microscope: a tube in which electrons are sent through an object and focused on a fluorescent screen. It is able to magnify the image much more powerfully than an ordinary *microscope*.

elver: a young eel.

embryo: an *organism* in its first stage of life in the egg, when its *cells* begin to multiply after *fertilization*.

endoparasite: a *parasite* that lives inside its *host*.

environment: the surroundings of any animal or plant.

enzyme: a chemical produced by living things which controls a particular chemical reaction. Digestion, for example, is controlled by enzymes.

evergreen: a plant that keeps its leaves all year round.

evolution: the way in which animals and plants change gradually over millions of years to suit their surroundings.

exploit: to use something for your own advantage.

extinct: no longer in existence.

fertilization: the joining together of male and female reproductive *cells* to start the growth of new *organism*.

fig tree chert: a type of rock in which the oldest known *chemofossils* have been found.

flagellae: microscopic threads used by some *protozoa* and *bacteria* to move themselves through water.

food chain: a series of living things through which food energy passes – a plant is eaten by an animal which is then eaten by another animal and so on.

foraminiferan: a type of microscopic animal, with a shell formed mainly of *calcium carbonate*.

fossil: the remains, usually the hard parts, such as bone or plant stem, of a living thing, which have become embedded in a layer of rock.

fossil fuel: fuel such as oil, coal and natural gas made from the remains of living matter.

fossilize: to turn into a *fossil*.

fungus: an *organism*, such as a mushroom or mould, which cannot obtain energy from sunlight like most plants, but lives on other organisms, alive or dead.

glucose: a type of simple sugar made by plants.

Gulf Stream: a current of warm water that flows up the Atlantic coast of North America and across to Europe.

habitat: the place where an animal or plant lives.

herbivore: an animal that eats only plants.

hermaphrodite: an individual *organism* which has male and female reproductive organs in the same body.

hibernate: to go into a long period of *torpor* during the winter to save energy.

hormones: chemical substances produced by plants and animals which stimulate action in other organs to which they are carried.

host: an animal or plant on which another *organism* lives as a *parasite*.

hydra: a small animal living in fresh water.

impression: the mark left behind when an object has been pressed into a soft surface.

insecticide: a chemical used to kill insects.

insulate: to stop the passage of heat.

invertebrate: any animal that is not a vertebrate. It does not have a backbone.

jet lag: the disturbing effect felt by some people after travelling by air over several time zones, so that although they may arrive in the evening their 'internal clocks' feel it is still morning.

kingdom: in scientific usage, one of the two main divisions in the study of living *organisms* – plants and animals.

krill: a small sea animal, like a shrimp.

laburnum: a tree with yellow flowers and poisonous seeds.

larva: the young stage of some animals, when they look quite different from their parents.

lek: a gathering of male birds where they display to attract the females to mate.

lemming: a small *mammal* living in northern grasslands.

lemurs: a group of forest-dwelling *primates* rather like monkeys.

lichen: a small plant which is really a combination of *algae* and *fungi*, living on tree bark and rocks.

lifespan: the length of an *organism's* life.

lodge: the home of a beaver.

luciferin: a substance in animals, such as glow-worms, which produces light when it is combined with an *enzyme*.

magnetic field: the area around a magnet where its force can be felt.

malaria: a disease, common in tropical countries, which results in fever. It is carried by female *mosquitoes*.

mammal: a warm-bodied animal, usually covered with fur, that gives birth to live young which feed on the mother's milk.

marsupial: a mammal, such as a kangaroo, whose young are born when very small and who spend their early life inside a pouch on the mother's abdomen.

membrane: a thin sheet, like a skin, which protects all or part of an *organism*.

metabolic rate: the rate at which *organisms* release energy from food.

methane: a gas, a compound of carbon and hydrogen.

microscope: an instrument in which lenses are used to magnify the image of very small objects invisible to the naked eye.

migration: the movement of animals from one place to another, often at certain times of year.

mimic: a harmless animal that gains protection by imitating a poisonous or fierce one.

mimicry: the imitation, by one species, of the colour, shape or sound of another.

molar: a back tooth of a *mammal*, used for grinding tough food.

molecule: the smallest unit of a compound substance, made up of several atoms of simple substances.

mollusc: an *invertebrate* with a soft body and, usually, a hard shell, such as a snail or a limpet.

multicellular: made of more than one *cell*.

navigate: to work out your position on land or sea, in the air or in space, and plot a course by which to travel.

nematodes: a group of small worms, such as threadworms and roundworms, some of which live in other animals as parasites.

niche: the position of a living thing in the natural community.

nitrogen: a gas which forms about eighty per cent of air.

nocturnal: awake and active at night, resting by day.

nucleus: the central, controlling part of a cell.

nutrient: a substance that an animal or plant needs to take in as food.

nymph: the young stage of some insects, before the wings and sex organs are fully formed.

offspring: the children, or young, of an animal.

organic: made of carbon compounds, which are the basis of all living things.

organism: a living animal or plant.

ovary: the part of female animals and plants where eggs are produced.

ovule: the 'egg' of a plant.

ozone: a form of oxygen which has absorbed ultraviolet rays from the Sun. A layer of ozone in the *atmosphere* prevents these rays reaching Earth and destroying life.

parasite: an *organism* that lives and feeds in or on another, different, organism.

pheromone: a chemical sent out by one animal that affects the way other animals behave.

photosynthesis: the process by which plants use energy from sunlight to make their food from water and *carbon dioxide*.

phytoplankton: microscopic, simple plants that float near the surface of fresh water or the sea.

plankton: the general name for all the microscopic *organisms* found floating in fresh water or the sea.

pollen: material produced by plants, containing male reproductive *cells*.

pollution: the act of making the environment dirty and harmful with rubbish, fumes and waste chemicals.

population: in scientific usage, the total number of individuals in a *species*.

predator: an animal that lives by hunting and eating other animals.

prey: the animals hunted and eaten by *predators*.

primates: the group of *mammals* to which monkeys, apes and humans all belong.

protein: an organic compound made mainly of *amino acids*, needed for the formation of *cells* and taken in, in food, by animals. Plants make their own protein.

protozoa: a group of microscopic, water-living animals each made of a single *cell*.

pupa: the stage during the life of some insects, in which changes take place to produce the adult form.

radar: a system for measuring the distance and direction of an object, by picking up pulses of radio waves reflected by it.

radiolarian: a microscopic animal with a skeleton formed of silica.

reason: to think logically, to work things out.

reproduction: the way in which all *organisms* replace their own species so that it will not die out.

reptile: a cold-blooded animal, such as a lizard or snake, which lays eggs and has a hard, protective covering of scales.

rutting: the fighting and display used by male deer and some other animals to attract females to mate.

scavenger: an animal that feeds on the remains of other animals, already dead when it finds them.

sewage: waste material carried away through drains.

sexual reproduction: *reproduction* of *organisms* by joining together male and female reproductive *cells*.

sieving: separating solid particles from a liquid, or smaller from larger particles, by passing through a sheet with holes in it.

social insects: insects that live together in large organized groups, and have developed different forms of the same *species* to do different jobs in the group.

spawn: a batch of eggs laid in water by fish, frogs or toads.

spawning: the act of producing and fertilizing *spawn*.

species: a group of closely related *organisms* which are able to breed with each other to produce young.

sperm: the short name for *spermatozoa*.

spermatozoa: reproductive *cells* produced by a male animal.

spore: a special *cell*, produced by some plants, which may grow into a new plant when it has been set free and carried away by the wind.

stigma: the sticky part of a plant where *pollen*, or wind, can *fertilize* the plant's *ovules*.

stomata: tiny holes in the surface of a plant leaf which let gases in and out of the leaf.

strychnine: a poison made from the seeds of various tropical plants.

symbiosis: a partnership between two different *organisms* which has advantages for both.

tarsiers: a group of small, forest-dwelling *primates*, rather like monkeys.

temperate: the word used to describe the climate in the regions of the world between the tropics and the polar circles.

territory: an area lived in by an animal with its family group, and defended against strangers of the same *species*.

thorax: the middle section of an insect's body.

torpid: in a state of *torpor*.

torpor: a state in which an animal's activity and the functions of its body (such as breathing) slow down to a minimum.

toxic: poisonous.

trilobites: a group of small, extinct sea animals, often found as *fossils*.

tundra: the level, treeless grassland found in the polar regions.

urination: the discharging of urine, the waste product from the kidneys.

uterus: the part of a female *mammal* in which the *embryo* grows until it is large enough to be born.

venom: poison made by snakes and some other animals to kill their *prey* and attack enemies.

vertebrate: an animal with a backbone, a skull, and a complex brain.

virus: a very small particle that needs to invade living *cells* in order to reproduce, and is the cause of many diseases in animals and plants.

vitamins: various substances needed by the body in very small amounts in order to stay healthy.

vitelline membrane: a strong *membrane* that surrounds the *fertilized* yolk of an egg.

womb: another name for the *uterus*.

zooplankton: simple microscopic animals that float near the surface of the ocean or fresh water.

Index

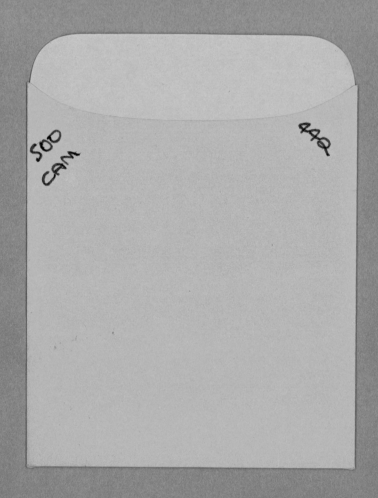

SOO
CAM

440

TE DUE

RAECO